GOTHIC ARCHITECTURE

THE GREAT AGES OF WORLD ARCHITECTURE

GREEK *Robert L. Scranton*
ROMAN *Frank E. Brown*
EARLY CHRISTIAN AND BYZANTINE *William L. MacDonald*
MEDIEVAL *Howard Saalman*
GOTHIC *Robert Branner*
RENAISSANCE *Bates Lowry*
BAROQUE AND ROCOCO *Henry A. Millon*
MODERN *Vincent Scully, Jr.*
WESTERN ISLAMIC *John D. Hoag*
PRE-COLUMBIAN *Donald Robertson*
CHINESE AND INDIAN *Nelson I. Wu*
JAPANESE *William Alex*

GOTHIC ARCHITECTURE

by Robert Branner

GEORGE BRAZILLER · NEW YORK

Library of Congress Catalog Card Number: 61-13690

Second Printing, 1965

Illustrations printed in the Netherlands
Text printed in the United States of America

CONTENTS

PREFACE

In a work endeavoring to present a concise analysis of Gothic architecture, many things of interest to the student of the Middle Ages must inevitably be omitted. It has been impossible, for instance, to discuss such aspects of the great Gothic cathedrals as their rich sculpture and stained glass, or their furnishings, which often included monumental choir-screens and elaborate stalls and altars. The reader may also wonder why nothing has been said about late medieval country houses, town houses and other civil structures, and castles. Restrictions of space form only part of the answer for these omissions. Military architecture in the Middle Ages seems to have followed a pattern of its own, whether in the eleventh century or in the thirteenth and fourteenth, and it is difficult, if not impossible, to find a point at which it ever took the lead in the development of features that can properly be called Gothic in the sense in which the word is used in this book. Moreover, many types of civil architecture remained remarkably traditional. Finally, the country house seems more important in the history of early Renaissance architecture than in that of Gothic.

I should like to express my particular thanks to my wife, to Mr. Adolf K. Placzek, Librarian of the Avery Memorial Library in Columbia University, and to his efficient staff, for their valuable assistance during the preparation of the manuscript.

ROBERT BRANNER
New York, April 7, 1961

For nearly four hundred years Gothic style dominated the architecture of Western Europe. Originating in northern France in the twelfth century, it spread rapidly across England and the Continent, invaded the old Viking empire of Scandinavia, confronted the Byzantine provinces of Central Europe and even made appearances, under the aegis of crusader and explorer, in the Near East and the Americas. By 1400 Gothic had become the universal style of building in the Western world, and it subsumed many types of structures. Gothic architects designed town halls, royal palaces, courthouses and hospitals (plates 99, 103, 104), they fortified cities and castles to defend lands against invasion, and they created bridges and hostelries to facilitate communication (plates 101, 102). But it was in the service of the Church that the Gothic style attained its most meaningful expression, for the Church was the most prolific builder of the Middle Ages, providing the widest scope for the development of architectural ideas and calling forth the best talents.

The transcendental character of medieval religious architecture was given a special form in the Gothic church (plate 1). Medieval man considered himself but an imperfect "refraction" of the

Divine Light of God, Whose temple on earth, according to the text of the dedication ritual, stood for the Heavenly City of Jerusalem. The Gothic interpretation of this point of view was a monument that seems to dwarf the man who enters it, for space, light, structure and the plastic effects of the masonry are organized to produce a visionary scale. There is no fixed set of proportions in the parts, such as can be developed from the diameter of a Greek column, and no standard relationship between solid and void. The result is a distortion: large as it may be in real size, the Gothic church becomes prodigiously vast in appearance. Such a visionary character expressed not only the physical and spiritual needs of the Church, but also the general attitude of the people and the aspirations of the individual patron and architect.

Gothic architecture evolved at a time of profound social and economic change in Western Europe. In the late eleventh and twelfth centuries trade and industry were revived, particularly in northern Italy and Flanders, and a lively commerce brought about better communications, not only between neighboring towns but also between far-distant regions. Merchants from the north and south met in central Champagne, for instance, at international fairs that were held at regular intervals throughout the year. Politically, the twelfth century was also the time of the expansion and consolidation of the State. Louis VI of France (1108-37) forced his recalcitrant vassals to acknowledge the royal authority and thereby laid the foundations of the kingdom that was to flourish in the next century, and only a little later Henry II Plantagenet brought order and unity to England and to his recently acquired domains on the Continent. Concurrently with these political and economic developments, a powerful new intellectual movement arose that was stimulated by the translation of ancient authors from Greek and Arabic into Latin, and a new literature, both lyric and epic, came into being. The heroic *chanson de geste*, in particular, gave the people at large a sense of their common European heritage. As a result of all these developments, the isolationism of the earlier feudal era gave way to a new, cosmopolitan world.

Gothic architecture both contributed to these changes and was affected by them. The dissemination of the style from its birthplace in the Ile-de-France, for instance—an important phenomenon which we will examine in detail below—was not unlike the exportation of an industrial technique. And in the thirteenth century, such an exportation easily reached the far corners of the Western world along the routes of commerce. But architecture is more than simply a technique. It has a permanence of its own, and it conditions the minds as well as the footsteps of the people who make use of it. Gothic was not dark, massive, and contained, like the older Romanesque style, but light, open and aerial, and its appearance in all parts of Europe had an enduring effect on the outlook of succeeding generations.

The Gothic style was essentially urban (plate 2). The cathedrals of course were all situated in towns, and most monasteries, with the notable exception of those of the ascetic Cistercians, had by the twelfth century become centers of communities which possessed many of the functions of civic life. The cathedral or abbey church was the edifice in which the populace congregated on major feast days; it saw the start and the end of splendid and colorful processions, and it housed the earliest dramatic performances or lent its façade to them like stage scenery. The abbey traditionally comprised at least a cloister, a dormitory and a refectory for the monks, but the cathedral also lay amid a complex of buildings, the bishop's palace, a cloister and the houses of the canons, a school, a prison and a hospital. And it dominated them all, rising high above the town like a marker to be seen from afar.

The architectural needs of the Church were expressed in both physical and iconographical terms. Like its Romanesque predecessor, the Gothic cathedral was eminently adaptable (plates 1a, 16a). It could be planned larger or smaller, longer or shorter, with or without transepts and ambulatory, according to the traditions and desires of each community. It had no predetermined proportions or number of parts, like the Roman temple or the centrally planned church of the Renaissance. Its social and liturgical obligations demanded a main altar at the end of a choir where the chapter and the various dignitaries would be seated, a number of minor altars, and an area for processions within the body of the edifice. There were rarely more than about two hundred persons participating in the service, however, a number that even the smallest Gothic cathedral could easily contain. The rest of the building simply supplemented this core and provided space for the laity, who were not permitted to enter the choir or sanctuary. Indeed, after the middle of the thirteenth century, the choir was usually isolated by a monumental screen that effectively prevented laymen from even seeing the service, and special devotional books came into vogue to supply the congregation with suitable subjects of meditation during the mass.

The more worldly and critical outlook of the twelfth century had an effect on the physical character of the Gothic church, as can be seen for example in the new approach to the cult of relics. Relics continued to be venerated, as they had been in the past, but they ceased to be the object of blind devotion, and they were transferred from the dim recesses of a crypt to bright, bejeweled caskets that were set upon stands behind the altar. The crypt, which had raised the sanctuary to a higher level than the nave, consequently passed out of use and the pavement could now be at a uniform level in all parts of the building. This was symptomatic of other changes tending toward unity of design. The ambulatory and radiating chapels around the sanctuary were inherited from the Romanesque period, but now the chapels were placed next to one another, providing an opportunity to integrate the minor volumes of the monument, and although the transept continued to be employed, it lost much of its architectural independence and was subordinated to the over-all scheme. In the largest sense of the phrase, the Gothic church emphasized the totality, rather than the complexity, of the concept of the Heavenly Jerusalem.

The program of the Gothic church fulfilled iconographical as well as social requirements. The intellectual centers of the Middle Ages had long been associated with the Church, and the tradition of learning that had been preserved in monastic and cathedral schools gave rise, in the late twelfth and thirteenth centuries, to universities such as Paris and Oxford. Such an association obviously had an effect upon the arts, which were still primarily religious in nature. Scholarly clerics, for instance, were delegated to devise the intricate, theological programs for the sculpture and the stained glass that adorned the church. The relationship is thought by some historians to have been even closer, for scholastic thinking first took shape in Paris early in the twelfth century, at the very time that Gothic architecture came into being there.[1] It is possible that architects, who were "abstract" thinkers in their own right, may occasionally have absorbed some of the habits of thought of the philosophers. In the absence of written documents, however, it cannot be proved whether these habits were consistently embodied in the design of the buildings.

Most of the symbolic interpretations of Gothic churches were written after the buildings had been erected, and therefore do not tell us what the original intentions of the patrons and architects were. Abbot Suger, for instance, whose church at St. Denis is the first Gothic edifice that can be dated precisely, was among the most articulate and interested patrons of the entire Middle Ages. In his two books on the administration of the abbey and the consecration of the church, he dwells on financial matters, on the ceremonies and the prelates who participated in them, and on the various metrical inscriptions he composed for the building and the stained glass. But he says almost nothing about the form of the edifice and its meaning to him, and if he equates the columns of the chevet with the Apostles, it is probably because they both happen to number twelve. In one place only does he seem to have invested the church with a specific and identifiable meaning, and that is in the façade, which was dedicated in 1140 (plate 3). Suger had worked closely with Louis VI in establishing the French State, and he advanced the idea that the Church was the spiritual defender of the realm. This had a particular importance for the abbey of St. Denis, which was not only the traditional burial ground of the Kings of France but also the holder of the *regalia*—the crown, tunic, sword and spurs that were employed in the coronation service. Suger seems to have embodied the concept of *defensor regni* in the façade, which is massive and is dominated by a crenelated parapet recalling the fortifications of a castle (plate 3).[2]

The Gothic cathedral forms a total experience that we can still understand today. The Cathedral of Amiens serves as an example. Begun in 1220 by the architect Robert de Luzarches, the façade of Amiens is dominated, like St. Denis, by two towers (plate 4). The buttresses run down to the level of the portals, dividing the surface into three vertical "bays," which correspond to the three aisles of the nave that lie behind it. The bays are intersected and tied together by two horizontal galleries and by the zigzag of the gables. The height of the side aisles is marked by the arches above and behind the gables—not very clearly or organically, it must be admitted—but the peak of the main vaults is filled by the great "eye," the rose window. To either side of the rose are pairs of arches, and only above this level were the towers originally meant to rise free and unimpeded. The regular vertical and horizontal divisions are not unlike those of St. Denis and form the so-called harmonic façade that is typical of French Gothic design.

14

The façade of Amiens is covered with decorative sculpture—blind arcades, pinnacles with crockets, and cusps. But more important is the statuary. Just below the rose is the Gallery of the Kings, representing the kings of the Old Testament, and perhaps also at the same time, the spiritual ancestors of the medieval Kings of France. The portals contain a more elaborate iconographical program, however, for in one sense they were considered the gates to Paradise, and in another they formed the area where the doctrines of the Church could best be displayed to the people. Each portal is dedicated to a specific theme—the central one to the Last Judgment, the one on the right to the Virgin and the one on the left to a former bishop of Amiens and a patron saint of the Cathedral, Saint Firmin. These last two themes are repeated on the transept portals, Saint Firmin to the north and the Virgin to the south. On the west façade, each tympanum is embedded in an array of sculpted archivolts, which represent angels, clerics, and subjects from the Bible, such as the Wise and Foolish Virgins. Each archivolt in turn surmounts the statue of a saint, angel, or prophet, beneath which are found reliefs of the Virtues and Vices, the Signs of the Zodiac, and the Labors of the Months. The themes are interrelated vertically, horizontally, and sometimes across the portal, from one side to the other. Thus the façade of Amiens serves both as a monumental frontispiece for the Cathedral and as the bearer of a complex statement of theological doctrine.

Most of all, the portals are wide and welcoming gates which draw the observer through the façade and into the building behind them. As we pass through them, we see the whole length of the monument laid out before us, the nave, the crossing and the chevet, which terminates in the hemicycle (plate 5). The axiality of the tall, narrow volume focuses our attention on the distant sanctuary. But we are not forcibly pulled to the east, as is the case in a Baroque church, since the lighting is evenly diffused from one end to the other (despite the loss of the stained glass), and since the spaces of the transept, which we cannot at once see completely, invite us to turn aside midway down the building (plate 5a). Furthermore, the sanctuary is backed by an ambulatory, which is lighted by the windows of the radiating chapels that are barely visible from the west. The spaces of Amiens do not form a single whole, but rather a series of parts subordinated to the over-all concept of a cruciform, basilican format. The interruption of the crossing provides a rhythmical interlude between the nave and the chevet, and the curve of the hemicycle brings the space to a conclusion.

On the exterior, the radiating chapels come into their own (plate 6). Elsewhere the plan of the Cathedral is rectilinear, but here, on the great curve of the chevet, the sharp faces of the polygonal chapels undulate in and out, pushing outward between the buttresses and echoing at smaller scale the dominating shape of the hemicycle. The exterior of Amiens is not a simple envelope that seems to transform the volumes into a solid mass, however. It is rather a half-open, half-closed composition of flying buttresses, pinnacles, and pyramidal roofs. If the interior volumes have finite limits, the exterior massing has no distinct beginning or end. The chevet is similar to the transept and to the nave in this respect, but it is only the flat terminals, with their portals, that provide access to the interior. The towers on the west façade, rising above the body of the church, indicate that the main entrance to the Cathedral will be found directly below.

It was Robert de Luzarches, not the bishop or the dean of the chapter, who designed the first part of Amiens to be erected, but both the patron and the architect collaborated to produce the building. One provided the specific program of the monument and the funds to build it, while the other formulated the design in detail and directed the construction. Many medieval patrons were gifted in architectural matters and could give precise directions to the architect, as well as appreciate the subtleties of his work. But their primary function was fund-raising and the administration of the project.

Building funds were assembled in several ways. Abbot Suger recounts how, when he began to construct St. Denis, he first inspected the abbey lands and put them in order, so as to insure a stable income for the work. By far the great majority of Gothic monuments was undertaken because of fire, and the patron therefore had no time to prepare the project properly. He sometimes directed certain Church revenues to the work for a limited number of years, generally three or five, but most of the money had to be sought among the nobility and the people at large. A disaster almost always brought immediate contributions from many persons, some of whom even joined the labor force for a short while as a symbolic statement of their attitude. But after the initial surge of piety had subsided, other means had to be found. The church relics would be sent around the countryside to raise interest in the project, and confraternities would be formed to nurture it by regular donations of many small sums. As a last resort, the pope would be requested to grant an indulgence to all those contributing to the work. Careful estimates of cost and time were difficult to make, however, and none but the most rudimentary of budgets could be established. As is still the case today, moreover, buildings must often have turned out to be more expensive than was anticipated.

The considerable size of many Gothic monuments meant that they were expensive to construct, and size sometimes also delayed the completion of the work (plate 7). But it is misleading to think that the great cathedrals took centuries to complete, for every major project was organized into sections or campaigns that were undertaken one at a time in a regular and predictable manner. When local interest was high and funds available, work was often quite rapid. Chartres, for example, was built in exactly twenty-seven years (1194–1221), and only minor parts of the exterior, such as belfries and spires, were not finished. Bourges was put up in two massive campaigns, the first from 1195 to 1214 and the second from about 1225 to about 1255; funds for the latter were probably assembled during the intervening years (plate 8). If financial problems arose during this interval, they could of course delay the work, and if the interest of the public and the patrons had waned in the meantime, the later campaigns might be put off for decades or even centuries. This explains the difference in style among the various parts of many medieval edifices, for each period built in the current style, and very few architects were disturbed by the juxtaposition of old and new.

The ultimate responsibility for the design and execution naturally lay with the professional architect. He was called a cementer, stonecutter or simply a master mason, epithets that reveal his intimate and enduring relation to the crafts. Since there were no schools of architecture, the mason had to learn his craft by participation, but he seems to have had a fairly thorough "course of studies" all the same. He was first an apprentice for four or five years, then a journeyman working in another shop for a year or more, and finally he became a master. Peter Parler, who worked at Prague in the mid-fourteenth century (plate 92), seems to have been a master by the time he was twenty-three, but one has the impression that his was a brilliant career and that the majority of Gothic architects were a good bit older and more experienced before they became directors of their own shops.

By the middle of the thirteenth century, the master mason had clearly become the head of his profession. He might take several jobs at the same time, like Pierre de Montreuil, who worked on Notre Dame in Paris and at the abbeys of St. Germain des Prés and St. Denis. He might also, like Pierre, own his own house and even some of the quarries from which he would then, in his capacity as architect, purchase the stone for a building. Most revealing of his new status, however, was the acid comment of the conservative Dominican friar, Nicolas de Biard, who wrote, "The master masons, with rod and glove in hand, say to the others, 'Cut it for me here,' and do none of the work themselves, although they receive the greater pay." This indicates that the Gothic architect had arrived at a level far above that of his Romanesque predecessor. From this time on he usually could afford a tombstone engraved with his name, like Hugh Libergier of Reims (d. 1263) (plate 9). Perhaps more important, the architect's work began to assume an identity of its own in the minds of his contemporaries. The names and activities of the successive architects who worked on the cathedrals of Reims and Amiens, for instance, were preserved for more than three generations and then inscribed in mosaic-like labyrinths laid out on the pavements of the naves (plate 10).

In Germany a veritable "cult" of the master masons developed in the fourteenth and fifteenth centuries, and the craft was organized into what must be called a guild. There were four major shops or lodges conferring the rank of master—at Strasbourg, Vienna, Cologne and Prague—and rules and regulations for the craft were drawn up and rigorously followed. One of the provisions was the prohibition against altering the work of a previous master in any way. At this time, economic problems sharpened by wars and plagues reduced the opportunity to build, and the requirements for mastership were consequently tightened in order to preserve the status quo. Only the son of a master could become a master, and the number of apprentices each could have was limited. This situation probably explains the widely held theory of the "secrecy" of the medieval mason, who was allowed to teach his craft only to a bonafide apprentice.[3] But such secrecy, which was first broken by Matthias Roritzer in 1486, seems to have been a late, and in some ways, a peculiarly German phenomenon. In Spain and Italy masonry was not organized in this manner; and in England and France, from the thirteenth century on, the craft was dominated, but not directed, by Offices of the King's Works.

18

One of the most interesting architects of the early thirteenth century was Villard de Honnecourt, a Picard from northeastern France. While no monuments can definitely be attributed to him, he has left us a manuscript, the only one of its kind prior to the fifteenth century to have survived (plates 11, 12, 13).[4] Villard seems to have begun the manuscript as a sketchbook and then to have turned it into a manual for the guidance of apprentices, adding explanatory phrases and directions to the drawings. Along with ground plans, elevations, and views of monuments, he sketched church furnishings, such as choir stalls, a lectern, and a great clock case. He also copied sculpture and perhaps even some images from stained glass, and he was fascinated by nature, drawing pictures of insects and animals. He included sections on roof-making, on mechanical devices—a perpetual-motion machine, saws, and levers—and of course one on masonry procedures. Thus the manual is a kind of summation, showing us how important the medieval master mason thought it was to have examples or models to follow, and also enumerating the many areas in which he might be expected to function competently.

One of the major responsibilities of the Gothic architect was the structure of the building. Whether it was large or small, simple or complex, the edifice had to stand, or it would serve no purpose whatever. Our clearest insight into Gothic solutions to structural problems is provided by the controversy that arose in 1386 at the Cathedral of Milan (plate 88).[5] The Milanese had begun an enormous church that seems shortly to have gotten out of hand. In their unfamiliarity with building on such a scale and in such a style, they were uncertain how big to make the piers or what form to give them. But most important of all, they could not decide how tall the piers, aisles, and vaults of the nave should be. They called upon experienced masters from France and Germany to aid them, and the visiting foreigners attempted to answer their questions by proposing that the shape of the nave should be determined by a simple geometrical figure. But each proposed a different one—an equilateral triangle, a series of squares, of rectangles, and a combination of these. The discussion, which lasted until 1401, brings into focus the principles of design employed north of the Alps in the fourteenth century. Proportion was almost an incidental question; what mattered was the over-all, abstract scheme or figure of the edifice, which the northerners called the "science" of building and which they thought helped to solve problems of stability. The fact that each master proposed a different solution indicates that these were not based on accurate statical considerations but were merely rules-of-thumb found to have been successful by generations of builders. Rodrigo Gil de Hontañon, the late Gothic architect of Salamanca Cathedral (plate 95), understood this approach quite clearly when he wrote that no master "appears to have established a rule verified by other than his own judgment."[6]

This is in marked contrast to the analysis of Gothic structure made only a century ago. For Viollet-le-Duc, the dean of nineteenth-century art historians, for example, the ribbed vault commanded the form and disposition of all the other members of the edifice, each of which was shaped with a view toward its function as a support; and the most important structural devices, in addition to the ribbed vault, were the pointed arch and the flying buttress. This theory was purely mechanical, however, and it also overlooked several historical facts. The flying buttress was not employed in all Gothic buildings—it was almost completely eschewed in England, for instance—and while the pointed arch was unquestionably useful in a Gothic structure, it was also employed in many Romanesque buildings, notably in Burgundy. And as the documents themselves indicate, the attempts of Gothic architects to make statical calculations in the modern sense were little better than infantile. More than a few churches collapsed during or shortly after construction, and those that stood were probably "overbuilt," with more masonry than a modern engineer would consider necessary. Gothic architects profited, not from their failures, but from their successes. On the other hand, it is clear on all counts that the medieval mason *was* concerned with statics in his own way. The evolution of structural schemes in the course of the twelfth century is in a certain sense like the development of a geometrical theorem, as Henri Focillon once said,[7] and we must therefore make a distinction between structural realities as they are now understood, and what the Gothic masters thought they were doing.

EARLY GOTHIC

Structure was, of course, closely related to questions of space, light, and plastic effects in the Gothic period, but there was no literary language in which these aspects of architecture could be discussed. We learn about Abbot Suger's theory of light, for instance, from his theological statements. Based upon the Neo-

Platonic philosophy attributed to Dionysius the Areopagite, who had erroneously been identified with the patron saint of the abbey, this theory argued that man could come to a closer understanding of the light of God through the light of material objects in the physical world. This accounts for Suger's interest in magnificent liturgical vessels of gold and silver and also for the extraordinary set of stained-glass windows with which he adorned the radiating chapels of the chevet of St. Denis (plate 14). He understood that stained glass had three basic properties: it was a bearer of holy images, an intrinsically rich material resembling precious stones, and a mystery, because it glowed without fire.[8] Standing as he did at the very point of the formation of Gothic style, Suger was able to impress the importance of light on succeeding generations of architects and to create a monument that was in this and other respects well in advance of its time.

Light was but one aspect of the chevet of St. Denis, and it seems to have been subordinated to the organization of space. This is suggested in the ground plan, which contains a choir and a semicircular sanctuary surrounded by an ambulatory and a series of radiating chapels that touch one another (plate 14a). The chapels are very shallow and open widely into a kind of second ambulatory, and each area is covered by a series of small ribbed vaults. But the parts were arranged in order to provide the maximum unity over the entire plan. The volume beneath each vault is not isolated and distinct, for the ambulatories and chapels flow together in a multiple but unified sequence, the wholeness of which is further emphasized by the thin, monolithic columns that simply mark off the vault corners. Light naturally pervades the farthest reaches of such a space, and as it comes from low windows placed along the entire periphery, the unity of the edifice is visibly enhanced.

Although it was not the generating element in Gothic, as Viollet-le-Duc would have it be, the ribbed vault was undoubtedly necessary to this conception. Technically speaking, the groined vault also concentrated the weight of the stone cover at the corners, liberating the walls from their function as supports, and it could also be twisted and subdivided to cover nonrectangular areas such as chapels. But it was thick and unwieldy, and clean, sharp groins on regular curves were difficult to construct. The ribbed vault, on the other hand, was simplicity itself, for the ribs were erected first, the number and shape determined by the number of supports and their distance from one another, and a thin cover, or web, of stone was then placed upon them. Pointed lateral arches could be used to raise the webs to any level, but in general the aim was a uniform height, approximately even with the central keystone.

ANGEVIN GOTHIC

Very shortly after the chevet of St. Denis was terminated, a totally different concept of Gothic developed in the Loire Valley, a domain of the Plantagenet kings of England. The Cathedral of Angers, the first monument of Angevin Gothic, is formed by a series of gigantic cubical volumes placed one against the other, each covered by a swollen, four-part vault that accentuates its individuality (plate 15). The wall is a massive enclosure, thinned only in the upper portion to hold a narrow walk and having two tall but narrow windows. Angers lay geographically close to the cupola churches of southwestern France where the same wall structure, with heavy piers and buttresses, was common. Influenced by Byzantine architecture, the cupola churches also had cubical volumes and naves made of a simple row of these gigantic units. At Angers, the position of the windows high above the pavement means that the interior of the edifice is not lit by a uniform, pervasive light, as is St. Denis. But here again prime consideration was given to the configuration of the volumes, to which structural techniques were subordinated, as at St. Denis.

Both Paris and Angers obtained the ribbed vault from Normandy, and ultimately from England, where it had been used in the Romanesque Cathedral of Durham (begun 1093). But the differing form of the vaults in the two early Gothic buildings announced at the very start the separate stylistic paths that each region was to pursue in the succeeding years. At Angers, the dominant feature was the very high keystone, which gave the vault a decidedly domical shape. At St. Denis, an effort was made to bring the keystone and the peaks of the arches more or less into line, so that one bay would be continuous with the next. The vault at St. Denis was actually no more "flexible" than the Angevin vault, but the architect made fuller use of its potentialities by bending it around the ambulatory or even by adding an extra rib to reach out over the area of the chapel.

The future of Angevin Gothic, which never became a directing force in northern French architecture, differed from that of St. Denis (plate 16). It consisted of expanding the volumes laterally.

This step was taken in 1162 at the Cathedral of Poitiers (plate 16b), which was related to a local Romanesque design with three aisles of almost the same height. Translated into Gothic, this became the hall-church, in which strong lateral perspectives replaced the normal oblique perspectives of northern France. Insofar as structure is concerned, however, Poitiers is fully as "Gothic" as its contemporary, Notre Dame in Paris. Each vault abuts the next one, so that the thrusts of the various ribs are all directed downward onto the piers, or taken up by large buttresses. The interior is thus liberated from divisions and becomes a series of similar cells developed in breadth as well as length. By the end of the twelfth and the early years of the thirteenth centuries, the fundamental concept of Angevin Gothic had been refined to an extraordinary degree. The vaults remained domical, and the ribs were multiplied in number and reduced in bulk, to form a network of thin tubes. On the one hand the piers were transformed into bundles of shafts, while the volumes were pulled upward, as at Candes (plate 17) and, on the other hand, the scale of the edifice was reduced to form a stone pavilion of exceedingly gracious proportions and effect, as at St. Serge at Angers (plate 18). But these two monuments represent the ultimate possibilities of the style. Light was still treated in the Romanesque manner and the wall was still a solid masonry enclosure. Only the vault continued to evolve, ultimately attaining the shape of a barrel with an overabundance of ribs, like later vaults in England (plate 19).

THE ILE-DE-FRANCE

The future of St. Denis was both more complex and more promising. The taller central vessel, with its several stories, provided a greater opportunity for development and was to result, by the end of the twelfth century, in the High Gothic Cathedral of Chartres. Suger's choir and sanctuary were rebuilt in the mid-thirteenth century, but the early Gothic Cathedral of Sens may, to a certain degree, reflect the original disposition of St. Denis (plate 20). Here there are three stories, with tall main arcades, a band of smaller arches decorating the area in front of the lean-to roof over the aisle, and a clerestory (also enlarged in the thirteenth century). This is the same general disposition as at Chartres, but certain important differences must be noted. The stories at Chartres are in better balance, with a clerestory much taller than the original one at Sens and very nearly as tall as the main arcades. In between, the triforium has been converted into a passage in the thickness of the wall, changing the simple, solid structure of Sens into one of voids (plate 7a). Furthermore, the great vaults of Chartres are much higher than those of Sens and are supported on the exterior by flying buttresses. At Sens there are six-part vaults and alternately strong and weak piers that divide the space into oversized compartments, each of which embraces two bays of the elevation and is flanked by four of the small aisle volumes. At Chartres, the vaults are four-part and every bay of the elevation is the same. Each main volume is flanked by two in the aisles, and the nave seems to be composed of a series of such "slices" placed next to one another. Finally, at Sens each story is expressed by prominent articulations of the masonry, such as colonnettes, arches, and horizontal mouldings, but the weak piers are smooth. At Chartres the plastic effects are more coherent, forming an over-all pattern that is roughly equal in all stories and that reaches down to embrace all the piers in the ground story. The clarity and regularity of structure, space, and plastic effects at Chartres express the order and balance of a classic point of view, whereas Sens, majestic as it is, reveals a more visibly complex, experimental state of design.

The line from Sens and St. Denis to Chartres was not direct, however, and the years between 1140 and 1194 were filled with a bewildering number of experiments. At first it seems to have been a question of catching up, for of the major buildings undertaken between 1145 and about 1160, none was able to achieve the unity and lightness of Suger's ambulatory or the compelling scale of Sens. St. Germain des Prés in Paris, with its heavy and still very Romanesque forms, is a case in point (plate 22); or the ambulatory at Noyon, where Suger's work was more closely studied and similar monolithic columns were used (plate 21); or even Senlis, begun in 1153, where alternation and six-part vaults were employed (plate 23). The results are all somewhat cramped, especially if one restores in his imagination the original short clerestory of Senlis.

THE EXPERIMENTS OF 1160-80

About 1160, when the chevet of Sens was nearing completion, early Gothic architecture underwent a profound transformation. On the one hand, there was a move toward gigantism, and on the other, a series of innovations in structure, plastic effects, and light, all of which were essential to High Gothic. Sens is a large building, but the need for a certain minimal size, in order to give full play to the effects of scale and to permit greater freedom in handling the configurations of the volumes, does not seem to have been generally realized for nearly two decades. Then, backed by interested patrons and with adequate funds, Gothic architects began to increase the size of their edifices until truly colossal proportions were attained. This can be seen in the presence of five aisles in Notre Dame of Paris (plate 24a), but its most vivid expression was in the conquest of height. Senlis was barely 69 feet tall, but Paris reached over 100 (plate 24) and the nave of Cambrai (now destroyed) nearly 115 feet (plate 25). The only way this could be done at the time was to add a fourth story to the elevation, and this in turn meant that the piers had to be strengthened above the level of the aisle vaults. To accomplish this, the tribunes were vaulted, and triangular walls, or sometimes even arches, were placed beneath the lean-to roof above them. The new story was placed between the tribunes and the clerestory and served once more to decorate the area of wall in front of the tribune roof. At Paris it consisted of a series of oculi, which were removed when the windows were enlarged in the thirteenth century and partly restored a century ago by Viollet-le-Duc. At Noyon, however, it was a band of blind arches forming a strong horizontal link between the bays (plate 26). It is hardly an exaggeration to say that these monuments were, to contemporaries, like skyscrapers turned inside out, with story after story towering up to the vaults.

The innovations in structure, plastic effects, and light that were made in the 1160's and 1170's, primarily in northeastern France, were equally important for the future of Gothic. The four-storied elevation of the chevet of Noyon, for instance, coincided with a Romanesque elevation that also had four stories but that differed in two significant ways: the tribunes and the main vessel were not vaulted, but the triforium had a wall-passage. Originating in England in the late eleventh century, this design passed to Flanders and thence to the Gothic monuments that were being undertaken at nearby Arras (since destroyed) and further to the south at Laon (plates 27 and 28).[9]

The importance of the triforium passage to Gothic cannot be overemphasized, for it represents a major step in the skeletonization of the structure (plate 27a). The wall was no longer treated as a solid support but was now hollowed out and reduced to two thin layers, one of which was further opened up by

25

arcades. The triforium also provided a dark zone between the tribunes and the clearstory and formed an additional space, like a slot, that gave further relief to the elements of the elevation. This is particularly noticeable in Laon, where the colonnettes and mouldings boldly stand forth from the face of the wall. And in the transepts of Noyon, which do not have aisles, the "wall" is in fact composed of three such passages, placed one on top of the other, the topmost one running along the exterior of the building (plate 29). It is obvious that here the vaults are sustained by the piers and by the masonry directly behind them that links the inner and outer layers of wall together (plate 29a).

A second step in voiding the wall was the multiplication of window openings. The replacement of masonry by stained glass admitted more light to the interior and transformed the wall into a screen, for the thin posts between the openings clearly do not have an important function in the over-all structural scheme. At Noyon each bay has two lancets, at St. Remi at Reims there are three (plate 30). Thus the fabric of the edifice was reorganized with a distinct differentiation between the supporting elements and the closures stretched between them.

These developments are succinctly gathered together in the chevet of the abbey church of St. Remi at Reims, which was begun about 1170. The elevation is ordered into well-defined zones, and each bay is subdivided from bottom to top into increasingly smaller units in the order 1:2:3, the six arches of the triforium in turn doubling the triplet windows of the clerestory. Furthermore the Master of St. Remi produced an unusually complex effect in the ambulatory by placing two columns in front of each radiating chapel and by reducing the piers between the chapels to the same form (plate 31). The ambulatory thus appears to be isolated from the chapels by a perforated screen, the spaces opening widely into one another. The conjugation of volumes, skeletal structure, and light in fact place St. Remi at the veritable climax of early Gothic design.

A third innovation in the northeast of France in the 1160's was the projecting transept flanked by both eastern and western aisles, which made the arms of the monument resemble the nave itself. In some cases, as at Noyon and Soissons (plate 32), the terminals of the transept were rounded, so that the church seemed instead to have three choirs flung centrifugally from the crossing. But it was the rectangular transept, with its four terminal towers, that was to affect High Gothic. At Laon, as later at Chartres and Reims, two towers flank each façade of the transept, and another rises above the crossing, to form a group of five that dominates the central area of the church (plate 33).

Still other advances of consequence for High Gothic were made in the 1170's. One was the invention of the flying buttress, which was first employed in the nave of Notre Dame at Paris shortly before 1180. If Gothic architects were unable to calculate precisely the weight and thrusts of a building, they nevertheless knew the value of certain structural devices. The Master of the nave of Notre Dame relied on the flying buttress to help support the vaults and roof, and he thinned the walls and the tribune supports beneath them. The architect of Mantes, who adopted the device during the course of construction, did not hesitate to reduce the outer wall of the tribunes from over five feet in thickness to a mere 16 inches, which left enough space for a small passage through the buttresses (plate 34). In both cases, however, tribunes continued to provide an additional brace for the walls and vaults well above the pavement.

Begun about 1170, Mantes has only three stories, and this marks the early rejection of the four-storied elevation, scarcely two decades after it had been introduced in Gothic design. The same rejection took place in northeastern France, but whereas tribunes were retained at Mantes, in this area they were suppressed and a new elevation was created, with a triforium passage in the central story. The oldest examples, such as St. Vincent at Laon, have since been destroyed, but the type survives in the slightly later church of St. Yved at Braine (plate 35). This was not yet the elevation of Chartres, but it contained the same basic elements—a main arcade, a triforium passage and a clerestory—and the structure was not dissimilar to that of High Gothic. The difference from the Sens elevation can be seen most clearly in a building closely related to the sources of Braine, the Cathedral of Canterbury in England. The central story of the first Gothic portion to be built, by William of Sens (1174–79), was merely a series of arcades opening onto the aisle roof, just as at Sens; in the second and slightly later part, executed by William the Englishman (1179–84), it was transformed into a wall-passage in the latest Continental manner (plate 36). In both parts of Canterbury, the clerestory passage that had become traditional in Romanesque England was retained, and thus in William the Englishman's work there are two superimposed passages, a little like those in the transept of Noyon.

27

With these disparate elements—the tall proportions of the nave, the three-storied elevation with triforium passage, the flying buttress and the reticulated surface pattern—the Master of Chartres created a new and unified design. Tribunes were unnecessary because large flying buttresses supported the vaults on the outside of the edifice, and the elevation was thus "liberated," while at the same time achieving great over-all height. The clerestory itself is very tall, descending well below the vault springers, and it contains large windows grouped into a coherent pattern. Moreover, the vaults are all four-part, the piers are of the same size, and each bay is outlined by prominent shafts that run down to the pavement. Regularity predominated in Chartres and was to have immediate as well as distant repercussions in Gothic architecture.

Perhaps the most powerful affirmation of the Chartrian scheme and the most complete expression of the classic phase of Gothic architecture was the Cathedral of Reims, begun in 1210 (plate 37). The general format of the building is the same as at Chartres, but the scale has been reinforced. The colonnettes and mouldings are larger and more vigorous than those of a twelfth-century edifice, and this impression is strengthened by certain changes from Chartres. The pedestals of the piers, for instance, are nearly at shoulder-height. This makes the whole monument seem much taller, or conversely, it would make a person accustomed to lower pedestals feel shorter in relation to the over-all height of the building. But the colonnettes are enveloped by large capitals that emphasize the horizontals at the expense of the verticals and increase the sense of weight and horizontality. At Reims perhaps even more than at Chartres, the calmness and stability of the High Gothic vision of forms are stated categorically. They are also expressed in the west front of Notre Dame in Paris (plate 38), where the nine compartments and two towers of Suger's early Gothic design at St. Denis were carefully balanced to give an impression of monumental peace. In a very definite sense, these High Gothic designs brought the varied experiments of the twelfth century to a term and opened up new horizons that were to be explored in the second quarter of the thirteenth century.

The impact of Chartres on thirteenth-century architecture must not, however, lead us to believe that this Cathedral was inevitable or predetermined, as two comparisons will show.

Almost diametrically opposed, for instance, was the concept of the Master of Bourges Cathedral, who began work in 1195, only a year after Chartres (plates 8, 8a). The Bourges Master also employed the three-storied elevation with flying buttresses, but instead of enlarging the clerestory downward, he drew up the piers to a height of 54 feet, exposing another complete elevation of three stories through the arcades, and he added two very low aisles at the sides, bringing the number up to five. The volumes thus pyramid upward, and the interior of the Cathedral forms a totality, all parts of which are visible from any point on the ground. This made Bourges inimitable, for the whole had to be copied or the concept would lose its meaning. This perhaps explains why it was never widely repeated, at least by the architects of the Royal Domain of the French Kings, who obviously preferred the more flexible scheme of Chartres. But in the west and south, at Le Mans and Coutances, and at Toledo in Spain, Bourges inspired a series of majestic variants that reveal the force of the original (plates 39, 40).

To northern French architects, the simplicity and imitability of Chartres were so attractive that another, slightly earlier concept was also driven from the field, to Flanders and Burgundy. Deriving from Trinity Chapel of Canterbury and from its northern French affiliates, this design—of which Geneva is an early example (plate 41)—retained the short clerestory but elongated the triforium instead. The Flemish masters of the second quarter of the thirteenth century preferred to place the clerestory passage on the exterior and to close it by a screen (plate 42), while in Burgundy it remained on the inside (plate 43). Notre Dame at Dijon is, in fact, one of the most spectacular examples of the style, for the main volume is flanked by lesser volumes in both upper stories, and the supports have been reduced to clusters of isolated shafts. Like Bourges, Dijon rejected the large, flat surfaces upon which the Master of Chartres drew the design of his elevation and which were to become the *terrain d'élection* for French architects of the first half of the thirteenth century.

With the nave of Amiens, the classic phase of Gothic architecture came to a conclusion (plate 5). The general framework of Robert de Luzarches' edifice was the same as at Chartres, but he introduced telling modifications. He reduced the bulk of the responds, thereby bringing the volumes into a closer relationship, and he reorganized the surface pattern of the elevation. The clerestory was now subdivided into four lancets with three rosettes above, as if each lancet in the window of Chartres had been invested with a smaller version of the whole design, and mullions and bar tracery replaced the regular, pierced masonry of Chartres. Bar tracery, in which long, curved pieces of stone are assembled to form intricate patterns, was henceforth to be a standard Gothic technique, providing an area for the display of virtuoso designs. Moreover, the triforium of Amiens, looking something like the one at Sens, was linked to the clerestory by tall colonnettes, so that both stories were tied together upon the flat surface of the elevation. The integration of once separate stories is perhaps the keynote of the 1220's, and the final step in the evolution of the idea was taken at this time in the aisle of Beauvais Cathedral (plate 44). There, not only are the triforium and clerestory merged into one another, but two small windows, now blocked up, were placed in the rear wall of the triforium. The elevation was thus completely glazed. The result of these developments was the inauguration of a new vision of forms.

THE RAYONNANT PHASE

Rayonnant design first came into focus in the years following 1240 in Paris. Named for the radial spokes of the great rose windows, it stands, however, for much more than simply a window form. With Pierre de Montreuil's work at St. Denis, speculation on the configurations of space virtually ceased, at least for the time being, and the massive scale of High Gothic was made finer and less substantial (plate 45). The heavy walls used at Chartres were now dissolved into glass screens periodically interrupted by very thin colonnettes, and the dark void of the triforium was completely lighted, to become an extension of the great windows. The vision of the building as a cage of glass is perhaps most succinctly expressed in the small Ste. Chapelle of Saint Louis, built in his palace in Paris, between 1243 and 1246, to house a fragment of the Crown of Thorns (plate 46). There the masonry, painted for virtually the first time in the Gothic period, all but vanished in the soft-colored light coming through the vast expanse of stained glass. Screening effects were also used on the exteriors of churches, as in the transept of Notre Dame in Paris, where paper-thin gables tie the façade together and lap over the adjacent story (plate 47). Gables were further used above windows, where they disrupted the firm horizontal cornice and altered the older effect of the wall as a simple envelope for the volumes (plate 25). Such an effect on the massing was of course implicit with the first flying buttresses, which added a half-closed volume to the exterior. But the glazing of the triforium meant that the continuous lean-to roof over the aisle had to be converted into a series of little pyramids, in order to expose the rear wall of the triforium (plate 6). The massing of the building was thus completely aerated in the 1240's, and the exterior henceforth became the scene of a series of fantasies that emphasized the fundamental illusionism of Gothic style.

From Paris, Rayonnant Gothic spread widely across medieval France and even beyond the borders. It appeared in the 1250's at Strasbourg (plate 48), which was modelled upon St. Denis; in the 1260's in Champagne and in the Midi, for example, in the extraordinarily elegant chevet of St. Nazaire at Carcassonne (plate 49). It also found its way to Burgundy in the 1270's and even to England at the end of the century, in the chapel of St. Stephen's at Westminster Palace, founded in 1292 (now destroyed).[10] With certain modifications, it was to provide the standard format of French Gothic architecture for more than a century.

GOTHIC ARCHITECTS ABROAD: ENGLAND

From the late twelfth century on, Gothic design was disseminated from northern France to the far corners of Europe. The first Gothic buildings erected in Germany, Spain, and Italy were frankly importations, more or less modified according to local taste and traditions. The Cistercian Order, which built in a rather uniform manner, also played a fundamental role in the spread of Gothic by carrying the ribbed vault abroad to the prodigious number of new foundations it engendered in the second half of the twelfth century. It was some years, however, before any of these regions was able to "digest" the new forms and to produce a Gothic design of its own. England alone, which earlier had been a kind of foster parent to French Gothic, at once adapted the forms to her own traditions, although even there French influences can periodically be discerned in the twelfth and thirteenth centuries. English Romanesque architects, with their preferences for strong linear patterns and for walls constructed in depth, had already approached a kind of Gothic formula, and the French ideas introduced at Canterbury between 1174 and 1185 touched off a movement that was from the outset clearly distinguishable from Continental developments.

It was the Frenchman, William of Sens, who was called upon

to rebuild Canterbury Cathedral after a fire in 1174 (plate 50). Having recently been in northeastern France, he brought with him certain ideas that were to become a part of English Gothic design for more than a century. The most significant was undoubtedly the use of detached shafts of dark-colored stone set against the light framework, a design that had been used across the Channel at Tournai, Valenciennes, and Arras . The contrast in color accentuated the differing functions of the colonnettes and the masonry core, and gave another dimension to the surface pattern. To this French design William added some English elements, such as the interior clerestory passage. In 1179, he was injured by a fall from the scaffolding and was replaced by another William (William the Englishman), who completed the eastern end of the Cathedral. As was noted above, it was he who transformed the false triforium of the central story into a wall-passage, in keeping with the latest ideas on the Continent, and by continuing to employ the clerestory passage, he set the steps for the developments in Switzerland and Burgundy that were to parallel French High Gothic design.

Perhaps the most original work of the late twelfth century in England, and one that points to a fundamental characteristic of English Gothic, is to be found at Lincoln Cathedral (plate 51). The monument was related in many ways to Canterbury, both in plan and elevation, but the choir vaults were laid out on an entirely different pattern (plate 51a). There is a ridge-rib running from east to west down the center of each vault, which shows that the crown is horizontal and gives the vault the appearance of a modified barrel. Moreover, the ribs of each bay meet, not at a single keystone in the center of the vault, but at two points equidistant from the transverse arches, and there are three on either side of the ridge. The result is a syncopated rhythm: the plan is symmetrical, not on the longitudinal and transverse axes, but on the diagonal one. Thus the ribs do not appear to have a logical function, and the bay is not brought to a climax in the vault. Even if this illogicality was the deliberate intention of the Lincoln Master, as has been suggested,[11] it nevertheless reveals the English preoccupation with over-all surface pattern rather than with the co-ordination of pattern, bay design, and volumes.

The English manner of building in depth can be seen in the early thirteenth century west façade of Peterborough Cathedral (plate 52). It is the antithesis of the Continental harmonic façade, forming a screen that is much broader than the nave behind it and that does not indicate the proportions of the vessels or even their number. At either end there are two small towers that scarcely rise above the gables of the central portion, and the latter is filled by three enormous arches of the same height that stand out from wall and cast deep shadows on it. There is a layered effect here, to be sure, but the splayed openings also emphasize the relief of the parts and give the impression of a thick but hollow mass.

The Cathedral of Salisbury, which was built on a site unencumbered by older buildings, reveals the persistence of English Romanesque ideals in the thirteenth century (plate 53a). The chevet is rectangular, with a single oriented chapel, the nave is very long, and the strongly projecting great transept has an aisle only on the eastern side. The smaller transept may have been an imitation of Lincoln and Canterbury, but it emphasizes the "loose" organization of the ground plan. There was no attempt to bring the parts together into a compact grouping; precisely the reverse, for the church, the cloister and the octagonal chapter house tended to spread out within the rather large, open areas of the close. Begun in 1220, Salisbury is in many senses the opposite of Amiens, its contemporary on the Continent (plate 53). Instead of towering upward, it is long and low, and instead of the half-open cage of flying buttresses, the various parts are smooth and solid, standing out with a sharpness and a clarity that recall Romanesque massing. There was to have been no focal point at all, for the west façade is a screen with towerlets at the ends, as at Lincoln, and the great crossing tower was created only a century later; but there is a unity in the repetition of the cubical masses of differing size and in the uniform decorative treatment of the walls, particularly with the doublet and triplet windows. In the interior, height was obviously eschewed for the more conventional English elevation with a tall, false triforium and a short clerestory, the latter of course with an interior passage (plate 54). It is quite apparent that the architect, Master Nicolas of Ely, was not absorbed by structural considerations and their visual expression to the same extent as was Robert de Luzarches. Flying buttresses were unnecessary in an elevation of only 81 feet and would have cluttered up the exterior. On the inside, the walls seem not to be paper-thin but quite thick, the various arcades serving to accentuate the depth of the masonry as well as to emphasize the horizontality of the edifice. The contrast in color provided by the dark Purbeck marble underlines both of these

33

effects. Furthermore, the bay division is minimized, because the vaults rest on small clusters of shafts suspended between the triforium arcades. This is all totally different from contemporary French design.

In 1245, King Henry III, who seems to have been much more interested in architecture than in administering his kingdom, began the rebuilding of Westminster Abbey (plate 55). The master mason was Henry de Reyns, quite possibly a Frenchman and a man certainly familiar with the Cathedral of Reims and with contemporary Continental design. His plan comprised a relatively short choir with an ambulatory, a ring of radiating chapels, and a projecting transept with aisles but without towers at the ends (plate 55a). The chapels, which have a narrow interior passage running above the dado, were closely modeled on Reims; but the towerless transept was a design that had come back into vogue on the Continent only about 1235–40, after Reims. French ideas are also to be found in Henry's elevation, combined with a strong dosage of English design. The clerestory is tall, for instance, the bays are delineated by colonnettes, and there are *piliers cantonnés* below. Flying buttresses also sustain the main vaults, but interestingly enough, there is only one battery rather than two, another development that took place on the Continent after Reims (plate 55b). Furthermore, while the triforium has an inner and an outer screen, it does not form a passage in the Continental manner but opens onto a deep tribune above the aisle that has its own windows and is covered by a low roof. The elevation seems flatter than was customary in England, while the spandrels are covered with a finely worked diaper pattern. The tall proportions of Westminster had a certain effect on later English buildings, but by far the most important aspect of the abbey church was the introduction of mullions and bar tracery in the window openings. From this time on, the simple designs of the Salisbury type were replaced by composed forms that became increasingly complex and far more fantastic than anything yet imagined on the Continent. How completely the composed window was assimilated in England can be seen in the octagonal chapter house of Wells Cathedral, from the early fourteenth century (plate 56). The rosettes and trefoils and the thin mullions seem to be natural partners of the rich linear effects of the piers and the dado, and the patterns have been extended to the profusely ribbed conical vault springers. Wells, Westminster, Salisbury, and Lincoln span a century of Gothic

34

design. Despite the movements and foreign influences discernible within this period, they all reveal fundamental similarities of approach to the forms of architecture that must be characterized as English.

GERMANY

No other country assimilated Gothic and produced a "national" design as easily as did England. But the isolation of this island does not completely explain the special nature of English Gothic design throughout the thirteenth and early fourteenth centuries, because Germany, which is contiguous with France and which had strong economic relations with Flanders and Picardy, also developed a particular interpretation of Gothic style. The new forms were introduced to the Rhine River Valley and then to the east in a rather regular geographic pattern. In the third quarter of the twelfth century, the ribbed vault was used in Alsace in an otherwise thoroughly Romanesque context, for example at St. Jean (plate 57). As in the first "Gothic" buildings built in Germany by the Cistercians, St. Jean should properly be called rib-vaulted Romanesque, for the walls, piers, and vaults are heavy and solid, without the apertures or the plastic effects that characterized early Gothic in the Ile-de-France. The rib did not have any consequences for the structure, and in fact it seems merely to have been another type of covering, like the groined or barrel vault. On the lower Rhine, particularly at Cologne, an architecture of voided walls had been developed in the second half of the twelfth century, but it was small and limited, and the addition of the ribbed vault, in the early thirteenth century, did not produce the same prodigious stylistic movement as the similar conjugation in northeastern France had some fifty years earlier.

From 1200 to the mid-century, western Germany was the scene of a series of importations. At Limburg an der Lahn, about 1225, it was the four-storied scheme of Laon, with tribunes, a triforium passage, and a clerestory (plate 58): The six-part vault was also employed, together with a simplified version of Aisne Valley sculptural effects. But the walls remained heavy, as if the Limburg Master were unwilling to trust the skeletal structure of his model. The result was a combination of French Gothic and German Romanesque, the one not yet assimilated and the other not yet outmoded. At the same time an Angevin Master was at work at the Cathedral of Münster, reproducing the great cubical spaces and domed vaults of his native style in western France

35

(plate 59). It is not only the movement of such architects across Europe that excites the imagination—that was natural enough in the cosmopolitan world of the thirteenth century—but also the fact that they often built in a manner long since out-of-date at home. Münster resembles Angevin work of the 1170's, for instance, and one wonders whether this was because the architect had been trained in a very provincial shop or because his German patrons wanted a replica of an older building they knew and admired.

A stylistic lag, of course, does not characterize all the early Gothic buildings of Germany. The nave of Bonn Münster (plate 60), for example, has three stories with two interior passages, like contemporary Geneva or Notre-Dame at Dijon; the five staggered openings in the clerestory resemble Saint Hugh's choir at Lincoln, just before 1200,[12] and other details recall nearly contemporaneous work at Arras or Bourges. Also related to the para-Chartrian style of Flanders and northeastern France is the Liebfrauenkirche at Trier, one of the rare central-plan buildings of the Gothic period (plate 61). The plan (plate 61a) was modelled on a small church in Tournai having diagonal chapels like those at Braine. The elevation has only two stories, with suspended verticals in the English manner, but the window tracery and the passage above the dado reveal a close connection with the High Gothic work at Reims and probably also Cambrai.

One of the largest German buildings of the entire century, the Cathedral of Cologne, was begun in 1248 on a purely French scheme (plate 62). The plan, like the one at Westminster, is typical of French ideas, and the radiating chapels were copied directly from those of Amiens, which were then rising from the ground (plate 62a). But everything at Cologne is pulled upward, and the vaults reach the astonishing height of nearly 160 feet, like the contemporary main vaults at Beauvais (plate 63). The upper stories at Cologne are similar to those at Strasbourg and St. Denis, linked together by common mullions in a four-part pattern, with a glazed triforium. Cologne is fundamentally an example of Rayonnant Gothic style on German soil.

It was at this time, however, after half a century of experience, that German architects produced a design that was to become perhaps the clearest expression of a national style. This was the hall church, of which the first example was the nave of St. Elizabeth at Marburg (plate 64). It is uncertain whether the concept of Marburg originated in local Romanesque buildings or in Angevin monuments such as Poitiers; certainly there are no Angevin details such as domical vaults or interior wall-passages at St. Elizabeth. The vaults are literally all at the same level, and the aisles are distinctly narrower than the main vessel. Moreover, the supports are *piliers cantonnés*, and the closing wall is thin and has two stories of windows. The result is much closer to a true hall than Poitiers, for the aisles seem merely to be extrusions of the central volume, and the impression of height is kept within bounds.

The nave of Marburg proved to be a spectacular success. In the course of the next three centuries hall churches multiplied throughout Germany, and the variations upon the original concept were as numerous as those upon Chartres. At first the proportions were lower, but later, particularly after 1300, they rose to achieve a fine vertical sweep with thin, svelte piers. The volumes were occasionally even enlarged by the addition of extra aisles, as at St. Severus at Erfurt, about 1270 (plate 65). The exterior generally formed a simple mass with a single pitched roof covering all the aisles, although it was sometimes composed of a series of small roofs placed at right angles to the axis of the building and terminating in gables above the aisle windows.

Yet the basilican format continued to flourish alongside the hall church in Germany. The nave of the Cathedral of Halberstadt, for example, has a tall clerestory rising high above the aisles (plate 66). This edifice is quite simple in design, especially in comparison with Strasbourg and Cologne, and it is likely that its severity represents the influence of the newer monastic orders, such as the Dominicans and Franciscans. But the slender piers and the shafts that rise directly to the vaults also convey a sense of tension that is a characteristic of Rayonnant design.

At the same time another movement began along the strip of northern Germany that borders the Baltic Sea and stretches east of Denmark. In this area were located the chief commercial cities of the powerful German *hansa* that traded with Scandinavia and Central Europe, and in the late thirteenth and fourteenth centuries one after the other of these proud, independent towns erected churches that are often quite similar in style. This is partly due to the fact that they are built of brick, the only material available in large quantity in the region. It is difficult to construct a Gothic building of brick because the statics differ from those of stone masonry, and thin, delicate articulations are virtually impossible. On the other hand a medieval brick wall has a surface that is softer and more modelled than one of dressed stone, and this is the chief characteristic of the Baltic buildings. As at St. Mary's in Lübeck, the masses are dense and the wall, of necessity, encroaches on the windows (plate 67). But therein lies the strength of the design, for it is a powerful architecture, drawing the utmost from the materials. Whether it was executed in brick or stone, however, mature German Gothic design of the later thirteenth and early fourteenth centuries tended toward spaciousness and simplicity of effects in the interior, placing richness and variety on the outside of the monument.

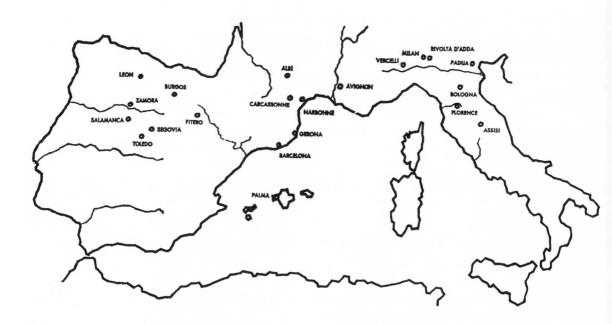

SPAIN

An independent interpretation of the Gothic style did not evolve in Spain until the end of the thirteenth century, and as in Germany, importations characterized the first hundred years of the style. Architects from Anjou and Burgundy, including Cistercians, brought the first Gothic elements to the peninsula. Angevin elements can be seen in the series of "Salmantine" lantern towers built in the last quarter of the twelfth century, which are named from the one at the old Cathedral of Salamanca. They have highly domed webs which are penetrated by the ribs, and the exteriors, with turrets at the corners and small aediculae at the springing line, are clearly related to French towers of the mid-twelfth century (plate 68).

The presence of Burgundian masters in Spain at this time is revealed by the Cathedral of Avila (plate 69). The Gothic building was larger than the Romanesque one and extended across the city wall, so that the periphery had to be construed as part of the system of defense (plate 69a). Within the heavy perimeter, however, Master Freuchal, the architect, placed a ring of shallow chapels around a double ambulatory much like Suger's St. Denis. The slender columns, composed of several monolithic shafts, confirm St. Denis as the model for Avila, although the more domed vaults and the rectangular arch section interrupt the continuity of the spaces. This is underlined by the separate vaulting of the chapels, and of course the very small windows, with deep splays, destroy the extraordinary effect of light that Suger's church had achieved. While this was occasioned at Avila by the thickness of the city wall, it was also a reaction to northern aesthetics, one which can be found in later periods of Spanish Gothic; for great windows were not essential in the bright Mediterranean sun, and with a few notable exceptions such as León, Gothic architects in Spain and in Italy found it more important to exclude light than to admit it. The slight rainfall meant that a tall, peaked roof was unnecessary; hence few Spanish buildings are dominated by this additional mass on the exterior.

The influence of St. Denis at Avila seems to have been transmitted through Burgundy, for the upper stories of the Cathedral bear an unmistakeable relationship to the church of the Magdalene at Vézelay, which was begun about 1185 (plate 70). There the original design included a choir of two bays, each with a false triforium like Sens or St. Germain des Prés in Paris, and with a four-part vault. During the course of execution the eastern bay was divided in two—one half was vaulted with the hemicycle, the other with a narrow four-part vault, and a six-part vault was placed over the western bay. A similar disalignment was effected at Avila, where both of the main transverse arches are placed above the centers of the main arcades, and the piers support only the minor ribs of the vault (plate 69b). The imitation of such an anomaly suggests a very experimental, not to say unskilled, approach to Gothic design and structure.

Early Gothic design in Spain also reveals some voluntary archaisms not unlike those of Germany. The Cistercians had employed the ribbed vault in the last quarter of the twelfth century, but when they constructed the abbey church of Fitero, after 1200, they returned to the scheme of Pontigny in Burgundy, of about 1150 (plates 71, 72). Both are almost perfect statements of rib-vaulted Romanesque, with heavy piers, solid walls, and a two-storied elevation, and an incontestable link between them can be seen in the capital, which is turned 45 degrees to follow the angle of the rib.

In the second quarter of the thirteenth century, inspiration by more nearly contemporary French models is indicated by two important Spanish cathedrals, Toledo and Burgos. Toledo is a combination of the five-aisled, contained-transept plan of Paris and the chevet of Le Mans (begun in 1217) (plate 73a). The latter suggested the alternation of four-part and three-part vaults of the outer ambulatory, together with the ring of radiating chapels, which are separated at Toledo by smaller, rectangular chapels. The flying buttresses are doubled in both, creating a bewildering aerial complex on the exterior (plates 73, 73b). But fundamental to both Toledo and Le Mans was the spatial concept of Bourges, with its five vessels of differing height. In the Spanish cathedral, however, the multiplication of piers from one ambulatory to the other alters the categoric relationships of French monuments, and the rather low volumes increase the effect of a labyrinthine interior, especially at the juncture of chevet and transept (plate 40).

The decoration of Toledo is heavy and ornate, revealing the influence of Moorish art, and the same quality can be found in the second large Spanish building of this period, the Cathedral of Burgos (plate 74). The elevation, piers, and many details indicate that Bourges was also the model for this Castilian building, although two of the aisles were suppressed and the staggered volumes were reduced to a simple basilican format. Furthermore, the tall triforium copied from Bourges was elaborated with a series of oculi, and the relieving arch was decorated with carved heads, the over-all effect again being that of Mudéjar art.

Reims and Amiens were the models for the last importation of consequence in early Gothic Spain, the Cathedral of León, which was begun about 1255 (plate 75). The ground plan and the form of the radiating chapels were based upon Reims, whereas the elevation was inspired by Amiens. León has the tall proportions and the flat surfaces of French Rayonnant, with a glazed triforium and great, traceried windows. But the design of the upper stories, with two narrow openings flanking the central group, goes much further toward deliberate compli-

40

cation and "illogicality" than anything at this time in France.

At the end of the thirteenth century, a new Gothic design was produced in northeastern Spain and the Balearic Islands. This area formed a distinct cultural entity, with its own language and a strong, sea-borne economy. Catalan Gothic was to a certain extent related to churches with single naves, such as Albi Cathedral (1282) in neighboring Aquitania, or the later Santa Maria del Piño in Barcelona (plates 76, 77). In both, the space forms an undivided, majestic whole. The walls are perforated by chapels that appear to be small and which, at Albi, are doubled by a second row above. It is difficult to appreciate the size of these buildings from photographs, for Santa Maria is nearly 65 feet wide excluding the chapels. Yet the effect of a colossal Gothic scale has not been lost in the openness of the space.

Several features clearly link Albi and the single-nave buildings to the Catalan basilicas of the late thirteenth century, among them the ring of chapels encircling the entire building and the absence of a transept. At Palma, there is one chapel per bay, but at the Cathedrals of Barcelona and Gerona there are two and at Santa María del Mar in Barcelona no less than three, whereas the nave of the Barcelona Cathedral has a second story above, like Albi (plates 77a, 78). The margins of the Catalan monuments are therefore fully as complex as those of the single-aisled churches. But the basilicas stand out because of their prodigious compound volumes. The central vessels are tall and surprisingly narrow in relation to the over-all dimensions of the buildings, but the effect of verticality is considerably reduced by the presence of very tall aisles. The vaults at Palma rise to 145 feet, almost as high as those of Beauvais and Cologne and significantly taller than those of Reims or Amiens, whereas the aisles reach nearly 100 feet, creating a very different set of proportions from those of French Gothic (plate 79). The Spanish buildings are not hall churches, for there is a small area of wall pushed up into the vault lunette, which bears a window and sometimes also a triforium passage. Thus the central vessel receives direct light, even if through rather small openings, and the aisles and chapels are lit by their own windows, so that the interior is pervaded by an equal illumination unlike either the German halls or the French basilicas (except, of course, the family of Bourges). But the emphasis was clearly placed upon the modeling of the volumes and the scale. The piers are slender—at Palma they are simple octagons—with the result that the volumes of the aisles seem to fuse with the central space. And although the bays of the main vessel are squarish and those of the aisles rectangular in a longitudinal direction, increasing the importance of the lateral perspectives, still a colossal scale is maintained by the rhythmic and close repetition of piers and vaults, so that the various elements are not allowed to fall back into set and predictable relationships. The smooth piers at Palma are a reflection of the impressive massing of these Catalan buildings, where flat, solid surfaces and sharp edges were used to great advantage (plate 80). The differing sizes and levels of the buttresses at Palma produce a rapid, contained effect that is a far cry from the fantasies of contemporary French Gothic.

The ultimate success of the scheme of Albi and the last great Catalan speculation on space is revealed by the nave of Gerona Cathedral, begun in 1416 (plate 81). There was some question as to whether the design should follow the many-aisled scheme of the chevet or the single-nave form. A group of architects was called in for consultation, and although a majority voted to continue the older idea, Guillèm Boffy, the chief architect, prevailed upon the chapter to adopt the single-nave plan. His judgment had been vindicated by time, for the vaults of the nave, which span more than 75 feet and are probably the widest ever achieved by Gothic builders, are still standing. But Gerona is not simply a tour de force; it is a final, supreme statement of the immensity of the Catalan vision of space which had been elaborated during the previous century.

ITALY

Italy, like England, betrayed a strong continuity from the Romanesque to the Gothic periods, but one that was modified by a constant return to ancient Roman and early Christian concepts. It was, perhaps, the particular situation prevailing in the Mediterranean peninsula which caused a special kind of Gothic architecture to develop there.

Italy had been one of the first countries of Western Europe to employ the ribbed vault. It appeared at Rivolta d'Adda (plate 82) as early as the last quarter of the eleventh century, but Italian architects apparently were not interested in exploring its potential and it was not pursued. A century later it was reintroduced by the Cistercians, but once again it failed to stimulate any changes in the structure or design of walls and piers, or in the body of the church as a whole. Just as in Spain and Germany, the thirteenth

42

century in Italy saw importations of French concepts. The church of San Francesco in Assisi, the mother house of the Franciscan Order, is as Angevin as Münster (plate 83). Although the vaults are no longer domed, the spaces are still cubical and the walls, which bear one of the most famous fresco cycles of the Middle Ages, have a narrow passage in front of the windows. Nearly half a century later the man who designed the chevet of Sant' Antonio in Padua revealed a knowledge of Bourges as well as of Cistercian and Franciscan monuments (plate 84). Despite these importations, however, Gothic did not take hold. The strength of Romanesque traditions is shown by the Cathedral of Siena, begun in 1269, in which the ribbed vault is practically the only concession to the northern style (plate 85). The elevation, with its two sharply separated stories, the piers and especially the striped masonry are continuations of a widespread and deeply rooted Italian tradition.

Three monastic orders—the Cistercians, the Franciscans, who were devoted to good works among the poor, and the Dominicans, who were dedicated to preaching—were perhaps even more influential in forming Italian Gothic architecture than they were in Germany or Spain. The cloistered Cistercians generally built simply and severely, while the Franciscans and Dominicans, who received great numbers of people into their churches, needed large buildings with good acoustics. But neither of the latter two orders employed elaborate designs or complex structures. The Dominican church of Santa Maria Novella in Florence, for instance, is simplicity itself (plate 86). The piers are still Romanesque, a rectangular core flanked by four engaged colonnettes, and the walls are flat and unarticulated. Even the arches and ribs are merely squared off. One can hardly speak of a bay design here, although the humped vaults tend to isolate the volumes from one another. Yet the main arcades are broad and open widely into the aisles, so that there is a vague reminiscence of the High Gothic manner of composing by slices.

43

The Franciscan church of Santa Croce, also in Florence, reveals a fundamentally new approach to Gothic architecture, although the forms employed were very old (plate 87). Only the apse and the chapels opening off the transept are vaulted, the remainder of the building being covered by wooden roofs. This is a version of the early Christian basilica, with simple walls above arches. The corbelled walk running below the clerestory has no more structural significance than at Siena, and the thin pilasters can scarcely be called responds, since they have no real function. The absence of any sense of "construction" here is indicative of the difference between Italian and northern Gothic. Santa Croce is actually enormous in size—the total width is greater than that of Reims Cathedral, the intercolumniation is also larger—but the apparent scale is not colossal. This was achieved by what must be called a "just measure." There are no parts, such as colonnettes, that are sufficiently small as to increase the apparent distance from one area of the church to another. There is in fact no network of shafts at all. Theoretically speaking, as the voids were enlarged to their present dimensions, so the solids were also expanded, as if both were controlled by some fundamental proportion. This was the Antique canon, distinctly in opposition to northern Gothic, and it prefigured the proportional systems used in the Renaissance.

A century later, when the Milanese were having problems of proportion with their Cathedral, the Servites, another mendicant order, began the church of San Petronio in Bologna (plate 89). This building reveals the distant influence of Santa Maria Novella, as can be seen in the elevation, which is slightly drawn up in height, and in the circular windows in the clerestory. There are, indeed, many Italian Gothic churches deriving directly or indirectly from Florence. But the proportional scheme of San Petronio is like that of Santa Croce. Everything seems to have a proper and reasonable size, and it does not seem to matter whether the building be large or small, for the parts and spaces would expand or shrink accordingly, always maintaining the same approximate ratio to each other. Thus if Italy made no significant contributions to the development of Gothic style north of the Alps, it nevertheless serves as a sort of yardstick by which we can gauge the extent and direction of that development.

44

LATE GOTHIC

After 1300 there was a general change toward more vertical proportions and the unification of over-all sculptural effects throughout northern Europe and Spain. This paralleled the phenomenon of cultural decentralization, the multiplication of artistic centers, and the loss of leadership by the old capitals. It was no longer simply the kings of France and England in Paris and London, but the popes of Avignon, Charles IV at Prague, the dukes of Burgundy in Dijon and Flanders and the duke of Berry at Bourges and Poitiers, who had their own courts and gave strong and continued patronage to the arts. Just before the middle of the fourteenth century the last two great German lodges were organized at Vienna and Prague. Two other events contributed to the general tone of Western Europe at this time: the outbreak of the Hundred Years War between France and England, which spelled the destruction of countless monuments in northern France and brought new construction virtually to a standstill, and the Black Death of 1347–48, which caused a grave economic crisis in the West and depopulated the shops of many of their architects and masons. These events do much to explain the general uniformity of Gothic style in the fourteenth century.

The Catalans were among the first to achieve a complete homogeneity of effects on a gigantic scale, as we have seen above, and a similar development took place in France at this moment. The abbey church of St. Ouen in Rouen, begun in 1318, recalls the French Rayonnant designs of the later thirteenth century, but it has a significant shift of emphasis (plate 90). The vessel is now tall and narrow, and the surface pattern more integrated. There is also a stronger interest in the effects of light and shadow. The front and rear screens of the triforium, for example, are deliberately disaligned so that the dark background contrasts with the light, forward tracery. The patterns of shadow cast by the tracery inside the building also begin to take on a new importance, and the deep colors of thirteenth-century stained glass are lightened and greyed, to emphasize the contrasts in monochrome. Therefore, although they may be very different in spatial composition and in details, the Barcelona Cathedral and St. Ouen have a certain common denominator.

England also participated in this development. The chevet of Gloucester Cathedral, for example, reveals an even more complex design than that which was coming to the fore on the Continent (plate 91). In the 1330's, the Romanesque roof and clerestory were removed, and the interior was sheathed with a fine screen rising to a higher level. Verticality is stressed by the innumerable mullions and by the rectangular panels in the spandrels of the arches. The vault is barrel-like and covered by a closely woven pattern of short, almost straight sticks. And the terminal wall is a prodigious glass enclosure in three sections, the outer two flexed as if to form a flattened apse.

At Prague, which was not affected by the plague, King Charles IV of Bohemia formed an important cultural center in the 1340's by hiring artists from various parts of Europe. For the reconstruction of the Cathedral, he called in Matthew of Arras from Avignon, and this master built the lower portions of the chevet (plate 92). When Matthew died in 1352, he was succeeded by young Peter Parler from Gmünd. Their combined designs are not unlike Albi or the more academic Narbonne (plate 93) in southwestern France. The main volumes are unified and the aisles have become much less important than they were, for example, in Amiens. The responds are connected to great sheets of tracery by oblique panels similar to those at Gloucester, and the wall seems to undulate from one bay to another. The tracery itself is consciously varied from one window to the next, providing many centers of interest, and the pattern of the vaults is striking. Simpler and more limpid than Gloucester, it represents, a century and a half later, the success of the irregular design of Lincoln.

The fourteenth and fifteenth centuries were also the era of the great towers, such as one finds particularly in Germany, as at Ulm or Freiburg. The tower at Strasbourg was begun in 1399 by Ulrich von Ensingen; it has recently been shown how this master drew the design out of the plan by a simple geometrical method (plate 94).[13] In fact, as the documents from Milan make clear, virtually all northern architecture of the period was laid out on geometrical schemes that were considered to insure stability as well as excellence of design. But this does not satisfactorily explain the effect of the Strasbourg spire. Rising far above the roofs of the town, it is a cage of tracery, with open spiral stairways in the turrets and others in the aediculae of the spire, an aerial fantasy representing the mystical aspiration of its designer and of a whole people.

If the great works of the fourteenth century represent a general re-orientation of aims, the forms used to express them were still those of an earlier period. The second and final phase of late Gothic, however, invented new forms and new configurations in response to still other drives. On the surface, the Gothic of the later fifteenth century seems to be nothing but a fantasy. But beneath lies a profound sense of contrast, a contradiction of traditional relationships that is characteristic of a baroque mentality and that marks a fundamental revolution in Gothic style.

The new Cathedral of Salamanca in Spain is symptomatic of a final revival of interest in the shaping of spatial volumes (plate

95). Gigantic in size, it has five aisles of staggered height, something like Toledo and the Catalan churches (plate 95a). But it differs from these in the emphasis on lateral perspectives and in its return to compartmentalized spaces. The piers are rather heavy and run up into deep arches that frame the bays, so that the walls become a series of recessed panels. The vaults, like most of those from the fourteenth and fifteenth centuries, serve as vignettes for the display of intricate, virtuoso designs. At the pilgrimage church of St. Nicolas de Port, in Lorraine, on the other hand, the simple basilican format was employed, but in contrast to earlier edifices, the aisles were drawn up in height and reunited visually to the central vessel (plate 96). The crossing is de-emphasized by slender columns placed at the opening of each arm of the transept, so that the lateral volumes there seem to be screened off. As a direct contradiction to the visual function of the pier as a support, the upper portion of one column bears twisted flutes, like the Baroque designs of the seventeenth century. In addition, the capitals have become useless, for they no longer mark the departures of the ribs and arches, which simply flow from the smooth columns. The same process can be seen in the exceedingly open hall church of Annaberg in Saxony, where the ribs also spring from the piers without articulated points of departure (plate 97). But here they twist and turn, forming graceful patterns on the surfaces of the vaults. This is another form of denying the rib its traditional function, one which is quite different from both Lincoln and Gloucester. Finally, at Henry VII's chapel at Westminster, the decorated conoids of earlier English vaults were replaced by traceried arches reaching up to inverted cones that are literally suspended from the vault (plate 98). The surface ornament serves to alter the impression of weight somewhat, but one cannot help feeling what was intended: that these great hanging keystones defy the laws of gravity.

The fantasy of late Gothic exteriors also reveals Baroque qualities. The Palais de Justice at Rouen, for instance, seems at first glance to be an example of *horror vacui*, so omnipresent are the decorative forms and the tracery (plate 99). But the flickering surfaces serve like a tapestry to conceal the massiveness of the masonry, and they unite all the parts into a whole. The complexities of buttress, balustrade, and gable indicate that the various parts have lost their distinctness as well as their original functions. The same general features can be found in the

47

Manoelino and Isabelino styles of Portugal and Spain, both of which are named for their respective sovereigns who played important roles in the discovery and colonization of the New World, Africa, and the Middle East. The portal of the Abbey of Santa Cruz in Segovia, for example, is rich in contrasts of solid and void and of light and dark (plate 100). Here geometric principles of design seem almost to have been rejected for sinuous, free-flowing curves. And above Vasco da Gama's tomb in Lisbon the ribs are carved as if woven of separate strands, like the ropes of rigging, and they form a sailor's knot in the crown of the vault over his head.

This was the last flourish of the Gothic style, for with the Italian Renaissance the Middle Ages came to a close. Gothic was the final expression of the medieval world, of the concepts of a mystical cosmos and a transcendental, universal religion. It marked the emergence of a cosmopolitan society in western Europe, whose increasingly elegant taste it was continually able to satisfy. But the essence of Gothic was most fully embodied in its conquest of space and its creation of a prodigious, visionary scale in the churches of the thirteenth century.

1. Chartres, Cathedral, 1194–1221. Nave.

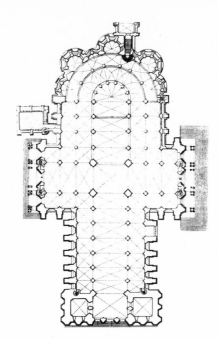

1a. Chartres, Cathedral. Plan.

2. Bourges in the fifteenth century, from the Book of Hours of Laval.

3. *St. Denis. West façade, consecrated 1140.*

4. *Amiens, Cathedral, begun 1220. West façade.*

5. *Amiens, Cathedral. Nave.*

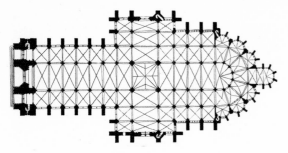

5a. *Amiens, Cathedral. Plan.*

6. *Amiens, Cathedral. Chevet.*

7a. *Chartres, Cathedral. Transverse section of nave.*

8. *Bourges, Cathedral, begun 1195. Chevet.*

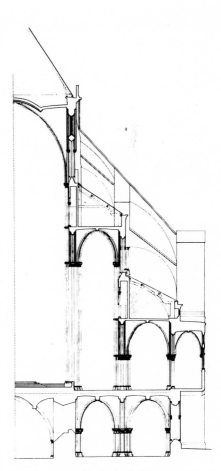

8a. *Bourges, Cathedral. Transverse section of chevet.*

9. *Tombstone of Hugh Libergier, d. 1263.*

10. *Reims, Cathedral, begun 1210. Labyrinth.*

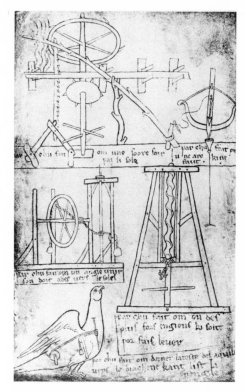

12. *Villard de Honnecourt, Sketchbook. Machinery.*

11. *Villard de Honnecourt, Sketchbook, ca. 1235. Choir stalls.*

13. *Villard de Honnecourt, Sketchbook. Tower of Laon Cathedral.*

14. *St. Denis, Ambulatories, 1140–44.*

14a. *St. Denis. Plan of apse.*

15. *Angers, Cathedral, mid-twelfth century. Nave.*

16. *Poitiers, Cathedral, begun 1162. Nave.*

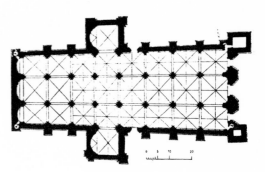

16a. *Poitiers, Cathedral. Plan.*

16b. *Poitiers, Cathedral. Section.*

17. *Candes, Abbey Church, ca. 1200. Interior.*

18. Angers, St. Serge. Chevet, ca. 1200.

19. St. Jouin de Marnes, Parish Church. Vaults, mid-thirteenth century.

21. Noyon, Cathedral, begun ca. 1145. Ambulatory.

22. Paris, St. Germain des Prés, ca. 1145. Side aisle.

23. *Senlis, Cathedral, begun 1153. Nave.*

24. *Paris, Cathedral of Notre Dame, begun ca. 1163. Nave.*

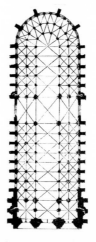

24a. *Paris, Cathedral of Notre Dame. Plan.*

25. Cambrai, former Cathedral, 1148–1252. Sketch by Van Der Meulen.

26. Noyon, Cathedral. Chevet, upper stories in execution after 1160.

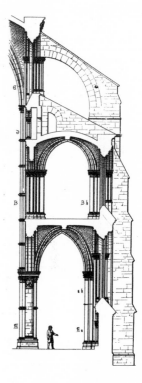

27. *Laon, Cathedral, begun ca. 1160. Nave.*

27a. *Laon, Cathedral.*
Transverse section.

28. *Arras, former Cathedral, under construction 1160. Sketch by Van Der Meulen.*

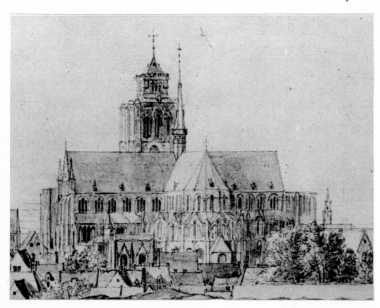

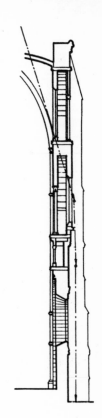

29. *Noyon, Cathedral. South transept,*
   planned ca. 1160–65.

29a. *Noyon, Cathedral. Transverse*
   section of transept.

30. *Reims, St. Remi. Chevet, begun ca. 1170.*

31. Reims, St. Remi. Ambulatory.

32. Soissons, Cathedral. South transept, begun in 1176.

33. Laon, Cathedral. Exterior.

34. *Mantes, Collegiate Church, begun ca. 1170. Chevet.*

35. *Braine, St. Yved, ca. 1195. Apse.*

36. *Canterbury, Cathedral. Trinity Chapel, 1179*

37. Reims, Cathedral, begun 1210. Nave.

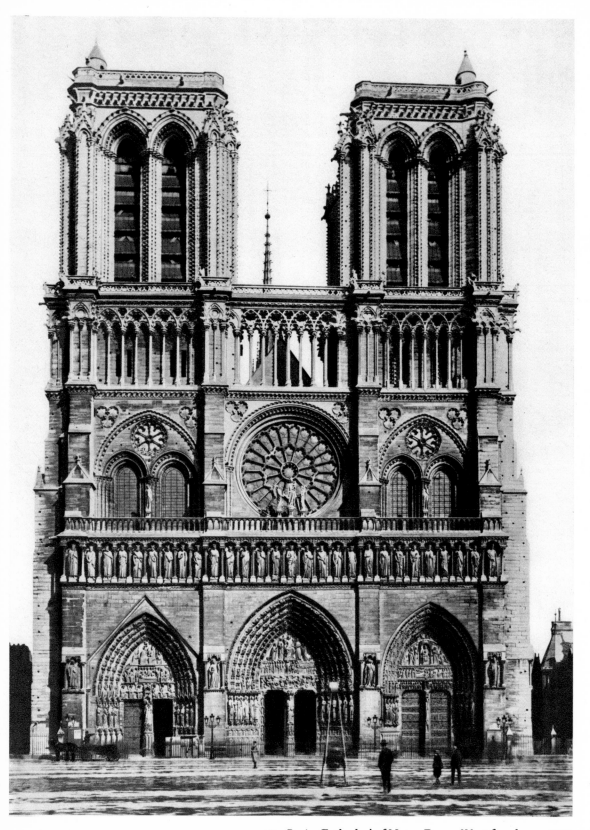

38. *Paris, Cathedral of Notre Dame. West façade, ca. 1200.*

39. *Le Mans, Cathedral, begun 1217. Ambulatory.*

41. *Geneva, former Cathedral, late twelfth century. North transept.*

40. *Toledo, Cathedral, begun 1222. Interior.*

42. Ypres, St. Martin, begun 1221. Apse.

43. Dijon, Notre Dame, begun 1220. Nave.

44. Beauvais, Cathedral, begun 1225. Ambulatory triforium.

45. St. Denis. Nave, mid-thirteenth century.

46. Paris, Ste. Chapelle, 1243–46.

47. *Paris, Cathedral of Notre Dame. South transept, 1258.*

48. *Strasbourg, Cathedral. Nave, mid-thirteenth century.*

49. *Carcassonne, St. Nazaire, ca. 1267. Transept.*

50. *Canterbury, Cathedral. Choir, 1174–79.*

51. *Lincoln, Cathedral, begun 1192. Choir vaults.*

51a. *Lincoln, Cathedral. Plan of choir vaults.*

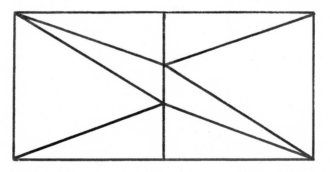

52. *Peterborough, Cathedral, early thirteenth century. West façade.*

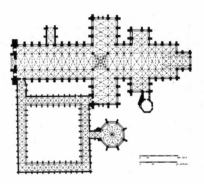

53a. *Salisbury, Cathedral. General plan.*

53. *Salisbury, Cathedral, begun 1220. Exterior from the east.*

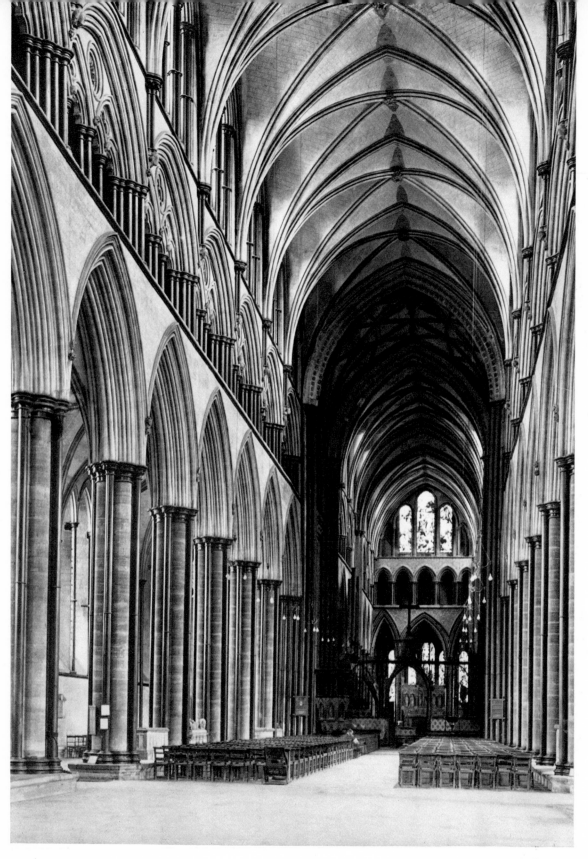

54. Salisbury, Cathedral. Nave.

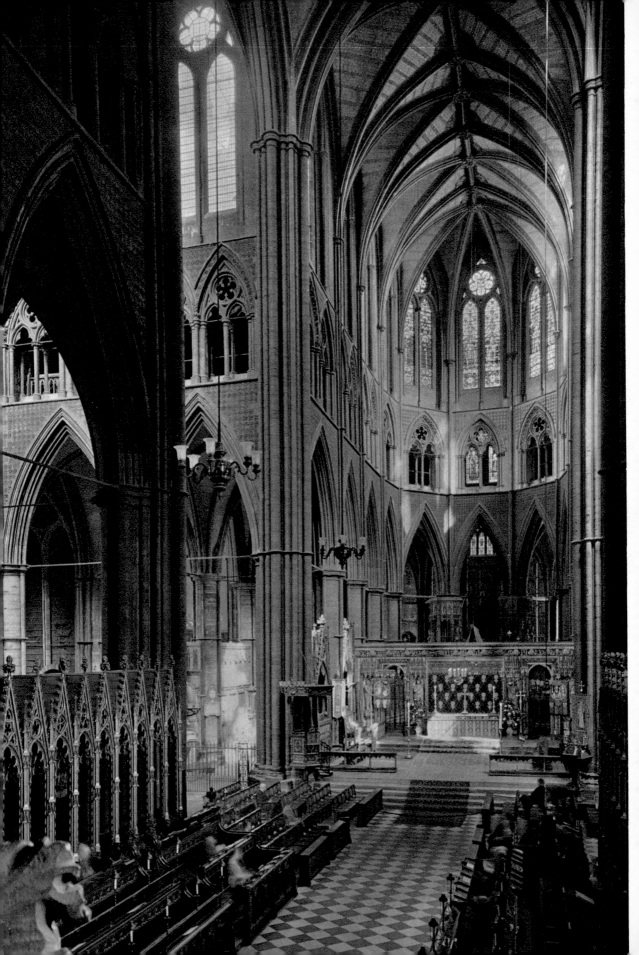

55. London, Westminster Abbey, begun 1245. Choir and chevet.

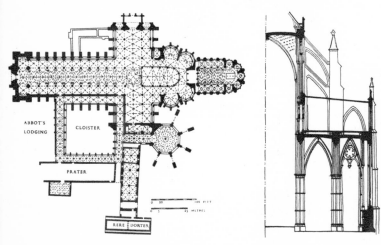

55a. London, Westminster Abbey. Plan.   55b. London, Westminster Abbey. Transverse section of choir.

56. Wells, Cathedral. Chapter House, early fourteenth century.   57. St. Jean, Parish Church, ca. 1170. Nave.

58. Limburg an der Lahn, Cathedral, dedicated 1235. Transept.

59. Münster, Cathedral, begun 1221. Transept.

60. Bonn, Münster. Nave, begun 1209.

61. Trier, Liebfrauenkirche, 1230's. Interior.   *61a. Trier, Liebfrauenkirche. Plan.*

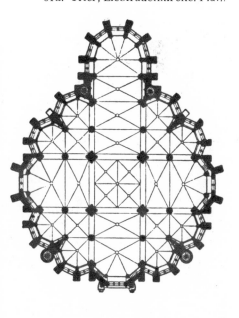

62. Cologne, Cathedral, begun 1248.

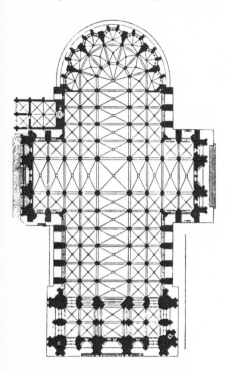

62a. Cologne, Cathedral. Plan.

63. Beauvais, Cathedral, begun 1225. Chevet.

64. *Marburg, St. Elizabeth, begun 1235. Interior.*

65. *Erfurt, St. Severus, ca. 1270. Nave.*

66. *Halberstadt, Cathedral, ca. 1260. Nave.*

67. *Lübeck, St. Mary, late thirteenth century. Exterior.*

68. *Zamora, Cathedral. Lantern tower, 1170's.*

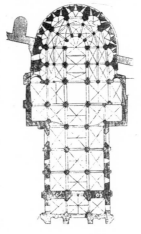 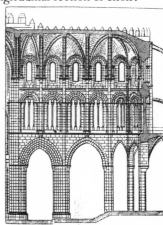

69a. *Avila, Cathedral. Plan.*

69b. *Avila, Cathedral. Longitudinal section of choir.*

69. *Avila, Cathedral, late twelfth century. Ambulatory.*

70. *Vézelay, Church of the Magdalene. Chevet, ca. 1185.*

71. *Fitero, Abbey Church, after 1200. Nave.*   72. *Pontigny, Abbey Church. Nave, ca. 1150.*

73. *Le Mans, Cathedral, begun 1217. Chevet.*

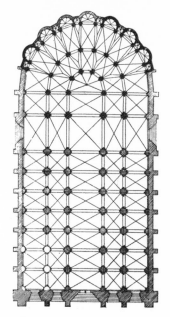

73a. Toledo, Cathedral, begun 1221. Plan.

73b. Toledo, Cathedral. System
of abutment of chevet.

74. Burgos, Cathedral, begun 1222. Nave.

75. *León, Cathedral, begun ca. 1255. Nave.*   76. *Albi, Cathedral, begun 1282. Nave.*

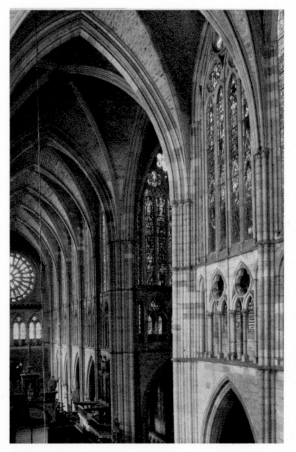

77. Barcelona, *Santa Maria del Piño*, early fourteenth century. Nave.

77a. *Gerona, Cathedral, begun 1310. Plan.*

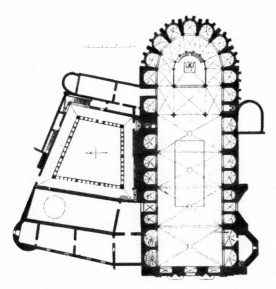

78. *Barcelona, Cathedral, begun 1298. Nave.*

79. *Palma de Majorca, Cathedral, late thirteenth century. Interior.*

80. *Palma de Majorca, Cathedral. Exterior, north flank.*

81. *Gerona, Cathedral. Chevet.*

82. *Rivolta d'Adda, SS. Maria and Sigismondo, late eleventh century. Nave.*

83. *Assisi, San Francesco, begun 1228. Upper chapel.*

84. Padua, Sant'Antonio. Chevet, begun 1232.

85. Siena, Cathedral, begun 1269. Nave.

86. *Florence, Santa Maria Novella, begun 1278. Nave.*

87. *Florence, Santa Croce, begun 1294. Nave.*　　88. *Milan, Cathedral, begun 1386. Nave.*

89. *Bologna, San Petronio, begun 1388. Nave.*

90. Rouen, St. Ouen, begun 1318. Chevet.

91. *Gloucester, Cathedral. Choir, 1330's.*

92. *Prague, Cathedral, begun 1344. Chevet.*   93. *Narbonne, Cathedral, 1272. Ambulatory.*

94. Strasbourg, Cathedral. North spire, begun 1399.

95. Salamanca, New Cathedral, begun 1509. Interior.

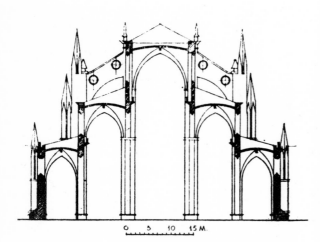

95a. Salamanca, New Cathedral. Transverse section.

96. St. Nicholas de Port, 1496–1544. Aisle.

97. *Annaberg, Saxony, St. Ann, begun 1499. Choir and chevet.*

98. London, Westminster Abbey. Chapel of Henry VII, 1502–20.

99. Rouen, Palais de Justice, begun 1482. Courtyard.

100. Segovia, Santa Cruz, begun 1482. Portal.

101. Avignon, Pont St. Bénézit, late twelfth century.

102. Carcassonne, thirteenth century. City walls.

103. Angers, Hospital of St. Jean, 1170's. Interior.

104. *Münster, Town Hall, mid-fourteenth century. Façade.*

NOTES

1. E. PANOFSKY, *Gothic Architecture and Scholasticism*. Latrobe, 1951.

2. S. MCK. CROSBY, *L'abbaye royale de Saint-Denis*. Paris, 1953, p. 35.

3. P. FRANKL, "The Secret of the mediaeval Mason," *Art Bulletin*, XVII, 1945, pp. 46-60.

4. *The Sketchbook of Villard de Honnecourt*, ed. Th. Bowie, Bloomington, 1959.

5. J. S. ACKERMAN, "'Ars Sine Scientia Nihil Est.' Gothic Theory of Architecture at the Cathedral of Milan," *Art Bulletin*, XXXI, 1949, pp. 84-111.

6. G. KUBLER, "A late Gothic Computation of Rib Vault Thrusts," *Gazette des Beaux-Arts*, XXIV, 1944, pp. 135-148.

7. H. FOCILLON, *The Life of Forms in Art*, trans. Ch. B. Hogan and G. Kubler, 2d ed. New York, 1948, p. 9.

8. L. GRODECKI, *Vitraux de France* (Musée des Arts Décoratifs, Exhibition catalogue). Paris, 1953, pp. 13-34.

9. J. BONY, "Tewkesbory et Pershore. Deux élévations à quatre étages de la fin du XIe siècle," *Bulletin Monumental*, XCVI, 1937, pp. 281-90 and 503-04.

10. M. HASTINGS, *Saint Stephen's Chapel*. Cambridge, 1955.

11. P. FRANKL, "The Crazy Vaults of Lincoln Cathedral," *Art Bulletin*, XXXV, 1953, pp. 95-107.

12. J. BONY, "The Resistance to Chartres in Thirteenth-century Architecture," *Journal of the British Archaeological Association*, XX-XXI, 1957–58, pp. 35-52.

13. M. VELTE, *Die Anwendung der Quadratur und Triangulatur bei der Grund- und Aufrissgestaltung der gotischen Kirchen* (Basler Studien zur Kunstgeschichte, 8). Basel, 1951.

SELECTED BIBLIOGRAPHY

(The following works are listed in chronological order of publication within each section; references given in the footnotes are not repeated here.)

GENERAL WORKS ON GOTHIC ARCHITECTURE

DEHIO, G. and VON BEZOLD, G. *Die kirchliche Baukunst des Abendlandes.* Stuttgart, 1897-1901. Two volumes of text and seven volumes of "measured" drawings.

KARLINGER, H. *Die Kunst der Gotik (Propyläen-Kunstgeschichte, 7).* Berlin, 1926. Has many illustrations and includes sculpture and painting.

CLASEN, K. H. *Die gotische Baukunst (Handbuch der Kunstwissenschaft).* Wildpark-Potsdam, 1930.

FOCILLON, H. *Art d'occident.* Paris, 1938. Contains fundamental chapters on Gothic architecture.

SEDLMAYR, H. *Die Entstehung der Kathedrale.* Zürich, 1950. Diffuse. See L. Grodecki's review in *Critique,* Vol. 65, 1952, pp. 847-857.

HARVEY, J. *The Gothic World, 1100-1600.* London, 1952. Contains an immense amount of information, sometimes a bit unreliable.

FRANKL, P. *The Gothic: Literary Sources and Interpretations through Eight Centuries.* Princeton, 1960.

SOCIAL, POLITICAL, AND ECONOMIC CONDITIONS

HASKINS, C. H. *The Rise of Universities.* New York, 1923; paperback edition, Ithaca, 1957.

HUIZINGA, J. *The Waning of the Middle Ages*. London, 1924; paperback edition, New York, 1954.

PIRENNE, H. *Mediaeval Cities*. Princeton, 1925; paperback edition, New York, 1956.

HASKINS, C. H. *The Renaissance of the Twelfth Century*. Cambridge, 1927; paperback edition, New York, 1957.

PANOFSKY, E. *Abbot Suger on the Art Treasures of Saint-Denis*. Princeton, 1947. Text and translation, with a brilliant introduction.

Cambridge Economic History, Vol. 2. Cambridge, 1952.

MUNDY, J. H. and RIESENBERG, P. *The Mediaeval Town*. Princeton, 1958.

THE GOTHIC ARCHITECT

KNOOP, D. and JONES, G. P. *The Mediaeval Mason*. Manchester, 1933.

HAHNLOSER, H. R. *Villard de Honnecourt*. Vienna, 1935.

PEVSNER, N. "The Term 'Architect' in the Middle Ages," *Speculum*, Vol. 17, 1942, pp. 549–562.

SALZMAN, L. F. *Building in England Down to 1540*. Oxford, 1952. An excellent account of working conditions, materials and men.

DU COLOMBIER, P. *Les chantiers des cathédrales*. Paris, 1953. Has excellent illustrations, largely from medieval manuscripts.

HARVEY, J. *English Mediaeval Architects: A Biographical Dictionary Down to 1550*. London, 1954.

BOOZ, P. *Der Baumeister der Gotik (Kunstwissenschaftliche Studien, 27)*. Munich, 1956.

GIMPEL, J. *Les bâtisseurs des cathédrales*. Paris, 1958; paperback edition, New York, 1961.

STRUCTURE AND TECHNIQUES OF BUILDING

WILLIS, R. "On the Construction of the Vaults of the Middle Ages," *Transactions of the Royal Institute of British Architects*, Vol. I, Pt. 2, 1842, pp. 1–69. Fundamental.

BILSON, J. "The Beginnings of Gothic Architecture," *Journal of the Royal Institute of British Architects*, series 3, Vol. VI, 1898–99, pp. 259–289.

LEFÈVRE-PONTALIS, E. "L'origine des arcs-boutants," *Congrès archéologique*, Vol. 82, 1919, pp. 367–396.

ABRAHAM, P. *Viollet-le-Duc et le rationalisme médiéval*. Paris, 1934.

MASSON, H. "Le rationalisme dans l'architecture du moyen âge," *Bulletin Monumental*, Vol. 94, 1935, pp. 29–50.

BONY, J. "La technique normande du mur épais à l'époque romane," *Bulletin Monumental*, Vol. 98, 1939, pp. 153–186. Important for the early history of wall-passages.

Le problème de l'ogive. Recherche, Vol. I, 1939. Articles by Aubert, Baltrusaitis, Focillon, Lambert, and others.

FITCHEN, J. *The Construction of Gothic Cathedrals*. Oxford, 1961.

FRANCE

VIOLLET-LE-DUC, E.-E. *Dictionnaire raisonné de l'architecture française du XIe au XVIe siècle*, 10 vols. Paris, 1854–1868.

SAINT-PAUL, A. "La transition," *Revue de l'art chrétien*, Vol. 5, 1894, pp. 470–482; Vol. 6, 1895, pp. 1–20 and 97–107.

GALL, E. *Die gotische Baukunst in Frankreich und Deutschland, I: Die Vorstufen in Nordfrankreich.* Braunschweig, 1955. (1st ed., 1925). On the twelfth century.

DE LASTEYRIE, R. *L'architecture religieuse en France à l'époque gothique,* 2 vols. Paris, 1926. The classical French textbook.

REY, R. *L'art gothique du midi de la France.* Paris, 1934. Southern France.

BONY, J. *French Cathedrals.* London, 1951.

VON SIMSON, O. *The Gothic Cathedral (Bollingen Series, 48).* New York, 1956. Primarily concerned with St. Denis and Chartres; see the review by S. McK. Crosby in *Art Bulletin,* XLII, 1960, pp. 144–160.

JANZTEN, H. *Kunst der Gotik.* Hamburg, 1957. On Chartres, Reims and Amiens.

BRANNER, R. *Burgundian Gothic Architecture (Studies in Architecture, 3).* London, 1960.

Many monographic articles will be found in the *Bulletin Monumental,* a series begun in 1834, and the annual *Congrès archéologique de France,* also begun in 1834.

ENGLAND

BOND, F. *Gothic Architecture in England.* London, 1906.

BONY, J. "French Influences on the Origins of English Gothic Architecture," *Journal of the Warburg and Courtauld Institutes,* Vol. 12, 1949, pp. 1–15.

EVANS, J. *English Art, 1306-1461 (Oxford History of English Art, 5).* Oxford, 1949.

BOASE, T. S. R. *English Art, 1100–1216 (Oxford History of English Art, 3).* Oxford, 1953.

WEBB, G. *Architecture in Britain. The Middle Ages (Pelican History of Art, Z12).* Baltimore, 1956.

BRIEGER, P. *English Art, 1216–1307 (Oxford History of English Art, 4).* Oxford, 1957.

Many short but clear monographs will be found in N. Pevsner's *Buildings in England,* a series begun in 1951.

GERMANY

DEHIO, G. *Geschichte der deutschen Kunst,* 4 vols. Berlin, 1921–1934.

KOMSTEDT, S. *Die Anfänge der Gotik in Deutschland.* Leipzig, 1921.

KRAUTHEIMER, R. *Die Kirchen der Bettelorden in Deutschland.* Cologne, 1925.

SWOBODA, K. M. *Peter Parler.* Vienna, 1943.

Short descriptions of the monuments will be found in G. Dehio, *Handbuch der deutschen Kunstdenkmäler.* Berlin, 1925–1928, (revised edition by E. Gall, begun in 1949).

SPAIN

STREET, G. E. *Some Account of Gothic Architecture in Spain.* London, 1865 and new edition edited by G. G. King, New York, 1914.

LAMPÉREZ Y ROMEA, V. *Historia de la arquitectura cristiana española* (2d ed.), 3 vols. Madrid, 1930.

LAMBERT, E. *L'art gothique en Espagne aux XIIe et XIIIe siècles.* Paris, 1931.

LAVEDAN, P. *L'architecture gothique religieuse en Catalogne, Valence et Baléares.* Paris, 1935.

MAYER, A. L. *El Estilo gotico en España* (2d ed.), Madrid, 1943.

DE CONTRERAS, J. (Marques de Lozoya). *Historia del arte española* (2d ed.), Vol. 2. Barcelona, 1952.

BALBÁS, L. T. *Arquitectura gotica (Ars Hispaniae, 7)*. Madrid, 1952.

ITALY

ENLART, C. *Origines françaises de l'architecture gothique en Italie*. Paris, 1894.

PAATZ, W. *Werden und Wesen der Trecento Architektur in Toskana*. Burg bei Magdeburg, 1937.

WAGNER-RIEGER, R. *Die Italienische Baukunst zu Beginn der Gotik (Österreichisches Kulturinstitut in Rom, Mitteilungen)*. 2 vols. Graz-Cologne, 1956–57.

LATE GOTHIC

GERSTENBERG, K. *Deutsche Sondergotik*. Munich, 1913.

GROOS, W. *Die abendländische Architektur um 1300*. Stuttgart, 1948.

INDEX

Numbers in regular roman type refer to text pages; *italic* figures refer to the plates.

121

SOURCES OF ILLUSTRATIONS

A. C. L., Bruxelles: 42

Alinari-Anderson, Rome: 83, 84, 85, 86, 87, 88, 89

Archives Photographiques, Paris: 1, 3, 5, 6, 7, 14, 15, 16, 17, 18, 19, 20, 21, 22, 23, 24, 25, 26, 27, 28, 29, 30, 31, 32, 33, 34, 35, 36, 37, 38, 39, 43, 45, 46, 47, 48, 49, 57, 63, 70, 72, 73, 76, 95, 99, 101, 102, 103

Arribas, Zaragoza: 40

Marcel Aubert, *La Cathédrale de Chartres* (Paris, 1952): 7a

Carl F. Barnes, II: 9

Bibliothèque Nationale, Paris: 2, 10, 11, 12, 13

Robert Branner: 8a, 44, 51a (drawing after Geoffrey Webb)

Fernando Chueca, "La Cathedral nueva de Salamanca; historia documental de su construcción" (Salamanca, 1951; *Acta salmantecensia, Serie de filosofia y letras*, IV, no. 3): 95a

Courtauld Institute of Art, London: 50, 51, 56

F. H. Crossley, Chester, England: 54

Georg Gottfried Dehio, *Die kirchliche Baukunst des Abendlandes historisch und systematisch dargestellt* (Stuttgart, 1887-1901): 14a, 62a

Herbert Felton, London: 55

Foto Mas, Barcelona: 68, 69, 71, 75, 77, 78, 79, 80, 81, 100

French Government Tourist Office, New York: 4

Ernst Gall, *Die gotische Baukunst in Frankreich und Deutschland* (Leipzig, 1925; *Handbücher der Kunstgeschichte*, II): 5a

Musée d'Art et d'Histoire, Geneva: 41

H. Karlinger, *Die Kunst der Gotik* (Berlin, 1926): 90

A. F. Kersting, London: 52, 53

Thomas King, *The Studybook of Mediaeval Architecture* (London, 1868): 1a, 16b, 24a, 27a

Élie Lambert, *L'art gothique en Espagne aux XIIe et XIIIe siècles* (Paris, 1931): 69a, 69b, 73a

Vincente Lampérez y Romea, *Historia de la arquitectura cristiana española* (Madrid, 1930): 73b

Robert de Lasteyrie, *L'architecture religieuse en France à l'époque gothique* (Paris, 1926-27): 16a

Pierre Lavedan, *L'architecture gothique religieuse en Catalogne, Valence et Baléares* (Paris, 1935): 77a

Photo Marburg, Marburg/Lahn, Germany: 58, 59, 60, 61, 62, 64, 65, 66, 67, 82, 92, 94, 104

National Buildings Record, London: 91

Nikolaus Pevsner, *Europäische Architektur* (Munich, 1957): 61a

Charles Seymour, *Notre-Dame of Noyon in the Twelfth Century; a Study in the Early Development of Gothic Architecture* (New Haven, 1939): 29a

Spanish National Tourist Office, New York: 74

Dr. Franz Stoedtner, Düsseldorf: 97

Tardy Frères, Bourges: 8

Theojac, Limoges: 93

Geoffrey Webb, *Architecture in Britain: the Middle Ages* (London: 1956): 51a, 53a, 55a, 55b

Westminster Abbey, London: 98